The Healthy
GLUTEN-FREE
Diet

The Healthy
GLUTEN-FREE
Diet

Nutritious and Delicious Recipes for a Gluten-Free Lifestyle

Abigail R. Gehring

Skyhorse Publishing

Skyhorse Publishing books may be purchased in bulk at special discounts for sales promotion, corporate gifts, fund-raising, or educational purposes. Special editions can also be created to specifications. For details, contact the Special Sales Department, Skyhorse Publishing, 307 West 36th Street, 11th Floor, New York, NY 10018or info@skyhorsepublishing.com.

Skyhorse® and Skyhorse Publishing® are registered trademarks of Skyhorse Publishing, Inc.®, a Delaware corporation.

Visit our website at www.skyhorsepublishing.com.

10 9 8 7 6 5 4 3

Library of Congress Cataloging-in-Publication Data

Gehring, Abigail R., author.
 The healthy gluten-free diet : nutritious and delicious recipes for a gluten-free lifestyle / Abigail R. Gehring.
    pages cm
 ISBN 978-1-62873-755-4 (hardback)
 1. Gluten-free diet--Recipes. I. Title.
 RM237.86.G44 2014
 641.5'63--dc23
                              2014002892

Printed in the United States of America

Contents

Introduction

If there's anything lucky about having celiac disease or gluten sensitivity, it's that we have it now, when the availability of gluten-free products is expanding at lightning speed. As few as five years ago, a lot of folks didn't even know what gluten was, and unless you were in a natural foods store or specialty grocery store, you wouldn't be likely to see a single item labeled "gluten-free." Now, many mainstream supermarkets have whole gluten-free sections, and many restaurants provide gluten-free menus! (Though, a word of warning: gluten-free menus are not always as exciting as they seem. I once ordered eggs benedict from a gluten-free menu, eagerly awaiting the first English muffin I'd had since discovering gluten made me feel lousy. When the plate arrived with just a lonely poached egg and a bit of hollandaise sauce—sans English muffin—I was sorely disappointed.)

Going gluten-free is a whole lot easier now than it ever has been before. Unfortunately though, many gluten-free products are not particularly healthy. Many are comprised mainly of starches and gums that are basically devoid of nutrition and saturated with unhealthy oils and lots of processed sugars. They may be "safe," but they're far from nourishing. My goal in this cookbook is to provide recipes for foods that are safe for those avoiding gluten and nutritious and delicious for anyone. Though some starches and gums are helpful for holding baked goods together in the absence of gluten, the focus of these recipes is on using a variety of whole grains and nut flours. Every gluten-free grain has its own unique flavor and texture that can be complemented with herbs, spices, or natural sweeteners like honey or maple syrup. These recipes aim to complement the grains' unique properties, rather than cover them up.

It takes some time to recognize which ingredients are safe and which are not. **Wheat, rye, and barley are the gluten-laden culprits you must avoid.** Unfortunately, that's not as simple as it sounds, since those three grains show up in a myriad of forms. Here's a list of common grains to watch out for:

Danger List: Ingredients That Contain Gluten

Barley, barley malt, barley extract
Bran
Bread flour
Bulgur wheat
Cereal
Durum
Einkorn
Farina
Farro
Gluten
Graham flour

Kamut
Malt extract, malt flavoring, malt syrup
Matzo
Rye
Semolina
Spelt*
Sprouted wheat
Wheat, wheat berry, wheat bran, wheat germ, wheat grass, wheat starch, wheat berries

*Spelt is an ancient variety of wheat, so it is not safe for individuals with celiac disease and is not used in any recipes in this book. However, some people with gluten-sensitivity or intolerance find that they can tolerate spelt just fine.

To further complicate things, these ingredients can show up in some unexpected places. The below ingredients do not always contain gluten, and when they do, it's trace amounts. But, especially if you have celiac disease, you should be careful about what brand of the following items you are buying. Look for ones that are specifically labeled "gluten-free." For a longer list, check out www.celiac.com.

Maybe List: Ingredients That *May* Contain Gluten

Alcohol
Artificial color
Baking powder
Brewer's yeast
Chocolate
Dextrin
Dextrimaltose
Dry-roasted nuts
Flavoring and flavor extracts
Glucose syrup
Gravy cubes
Ground spices
Instant coffee
Maltose

Miso
Modfied food starch
Non-dairy creamer
Oats, oat bran, oat fiber, oat syrup*
Rice malt
Rice syrup, brown rice syrup**
Seitan
Soba noodles
Soy sauce
Stock cubes
Teriyaki sauce
Vegetable broth

*Oats do not actually contain gluten, but are often processed in facilities that also process wheat. Look for certified gluten-free oats to ensure they're safe.
**Rice syrup is often processed using barley enzymes. Check with the manufacturer to ensure the brand you use is safe.

And now for the good news. Here are the exciting grains and starches that are gluten-free! To be sure your grains are not processed in facilities that also process wheat or other unsafe grains, still look for those specifically labeled "gluten-free."

Safe List: Grains That Don't Contain Gluten

Agar-agar
Almond flour
Amaranth
Arrowroot flour or starch
Buckwheat flour
Cashew flour
Chestnut flour
Chickpea/garbanzo flour
Coconut flour
Cornmeal and cornstarch
Flaxseeds
Gelatin
Millet flour

Oats (if they're certified gluten-free)
Pecan flour
Potato flour
Potato starch
Quinoa
Rice flour, brown rice flour, sweet rice flour
Sorghum
Soy flour
Sweet potato/yam flour
Tapioca flour and tapioca starch
Teff flour
Xanthan gum

Tips for Successful Gluten-Free Baking

- Use a mix of flours and starches. On page 3 you'll find a basic recipe for all-purpose gluten-free flour. It includes a variety of flours and starches, which helps to ensure a nice texture in your finished dessert. Using sweet rice flour adds some "stickiness" to your batter or dough that is sometimes lacking in gluten-free flours. I recommend brown sweet rice flour (rather than white), since it's a bit more nutritious. (Note: sweet rice flour is sometimes called "sweet rice glutinous flour," but it doesn't contain any gluten.)

- Go small. Smaller cakes, muffins, and cookies hang together more easily than really big ones.

- Add moisture. Applesauce, pumpkin purée, and yogurt add moisture and nutrition to gluten-free baked goods. Using brown sugar instead of white also helps, as does using a little honey, maple syrup, or gluten-free brown rice syrup.

- Chill your cookie dough. Gluten-free cookie dough tends to spread out a lot. This will happen less if you drop your cookie dough onto the pan and then stick the whole pan in the refrigerator for half an hour or so before baking.

- Darker baking pans will lead to better browning.

- Store your baked goods in the refrigerator or freezer to keep them from getting stale.

- One man's baking disaster is another man's gorgeous trifle. There are plenty of good uses for baked goods that fall apart, including trifles and cake pops!

All About Grains

Trying New Grains

Be adventurous with your gluten-free diet! By incorporating a variety of grains, you'll be more likely to get the nutrition your body needs to thrive. Here are some exciting grains to get acquainted with:

FLOUR	DESCRIPTION
Amaranth	Made from seeds of amaranth plants. Very high in fiber and iron.
Arrowroot	Made from the ground-up root. Clear when cooked, which makes it perfect for thickening soups or sauces.
Buckwheat	Highly nutritious with a slightly nutty flavor.
Chickpea	Made from ground chickpeas. Used frequently in Indian, Middle Eastern, and some French Provençal cooking.
Oat	Gluten-free, though oats are sometimes grown near wheat or processed in facilities that also process wheat. Look for certified gluten-free oats. Oat flour is just ground oats. High in fiber.
Quinoa	Made from ground quinoa, a grain native to the Andes in South America. Slightly yellow or ivory-colored with a mild nutty flavor. Very high in protein.
Soy	Made from ground soybeans. High in protein and fiber.
Tapioca	Made from the cassava plant. Starchy and slightly sweet. Generally used for thickening soups or puddings, but can also be used along with other flours in baked goods.
Teff	Higher protein content than wheat and full of fiber, iron, calcium, and thiamin.

Growing and Threshing Your Own Grains

Grains are a type of grass, and they grow almost as easily as the grass in your yard does. If you have the space, growing your own will save money—you've probably figured out by now that most gluten-free flours are pricey, but seeds are relatively inexpensive. Growing grains requires much less work than growing a vegetable garden, though getting the grains from the field to the table requires a bit more work.

Decide which grain to grow. Most cereal grains have a spring variety and a winter variety. Winter grains are often preferred because they are more nutritious than spring varieties and are less affected by weeds in the spring. If you have trouble finding smaller amounts of seeds to purchase from seed supply houses, try health food stores. They often have bins full of grains you can buy in bulk for eating, and they work just as well for planting, as long as you know what variety of grain you're buying. Winter grains should be planted from late September to mid-October, after most insects have disappeared but before the hard frosts set in. Spring grains should be planted in early spring.

1. Decide how much grain you want to grow. Refer to the chart on page xix.

2. Prepare the soil. Rototill or use a shovel to turn over the earth, remove any stones or weeds, and make the plot as even as possible using a garden rake.

3. Sprinkle the seeds over the entire plot. How much seed you use will depend on the grain (refer to the chart). Aim to plant about one seed per square inch. Rake over the plot to cover all the seeds with earth.

4. Water the seeds immediately after planting and then about once a month throughout the growing season if there's not adequate rainfall.

5. When the grain is golden with a few streaks of green left, it's ready for harvest. For winter grains, harvest is usually ready in June or July. To cut the grains, use a scythe, machete, or other sharp knife, and cut near the base of the stems. Gather the grains into bundles, tie them with twine, and stand them upright in the plot to finish ripening. Lean three or four bundles together to keep them from falling over. If there is danger of rain, move the sheaves into a barn or other covered area to prevent them from molding. Once all the green has turned to gold, the grains are ready for threshing.

6. The simplest way to thresh is to grasp a bunch of stalks and beat it around the inside of a barrel, heads facing down. The grain will fall right off the stalks. Alternatively, you can lay the stalks down on a hard surface covered by an old sheet and beat the seed heads with a broom or baseball bat. Discard (or compost) the stalks. If there is enough breeze, the chaff will blow away, leaving only the grains. You can also pour the grain and chaff back and forth between two barrels and allow the wind (which can be supplied by a fan if necessary) to blow away the chaff.

7. Store grain in a covered metal trash can or a wooden bin. Be sure it is kept completely dry and that no rodents can get in. To turn the grain berries into flour, see page xx.

Grain Growing Chart

Type of Grain	Amount of Seed per Acre (in pounds)	Grain Yield per Acre (in bushels)	Characteristics and Uses
Amaranth	1	125	Very tolerant of arid environments. High in protein and gluten-free. Use in baking or animal feed.
Buckwheat	50	20 to 30	Matures rapidly (60 to 90 days). Rich, nutty flavor perfect for baking and in pancakes.
Field corn	6 to 8	180 to 190	Use in animal feed, corn starch, hominy, and grits.
Grain sorghum	2 to 8	70 to 100	Drought tolerant. Use in animal feed or in baking.
Oats	80	70 to 100	Thrive in cool, moist climates. High in protein. Use in animal feed, baking, or as a breakfast cereal.

Milling Your Own Grains

Whether you grow your own grains or buy them whole from a health food store, you'll need to grind them into flour before you can cook or bake with them. You can grind grains into flour at home using a mortar and pestle, a coffee or spice mill, manual or electric food grinders, a blender, or a food processor. Grains with a shell (such as quinoa) should be rinsed and dried before milling to remove the layer of resin from the outer shell that can impart a bitter taste to your flour. Rinse the grains thoroughly in a colander or mesh strainer, then spread them on a paper or cloth towel to absorb the extra moisture. Transfer to a baking sheet and allow to air dry completely (to speed this process you can put them in a very low oven for a few minutes). When the grains are dry, they're ready to be ground.

Other Ingredients (Besides Grains)

Produce

Honestly, I can't remember a time when I didn't love vegetables. As a young girl I'd walk barefoot through our family's garden, snip pea pods off their vines with my little fingernails, and pop them in my mouth like candy. They tasted like sweet summer rains and crunched the way only something really fresh can. If you're skeptical of the locavore movement, you probably haven't tasted fruits and vegetables that have just been picked. They're like completely different foods than the produce that's been shipped thousands of miles to your supermarket shelves.

That said, we don't all have our own gardens. And sometimes even buying local produce isn't practical. But if possible, choose organic. Even if you wash your fruits and vegetables thoroughly, they will have absorbed some of the pesticides and herbicides used on the fields they were grown in, and for all kinds of reasons you don't want to put that stuff in your body. Also, produce that is not grown organically will often contain smaller amounts of the vitamins and minerals your body needs. If your budget won't allow all organic produce, at least choose organic for the following, whenever possible: apples, bell peppers, kale, lettuce, zucchini, nectarines, and peaches. These are at the highest risk for pesticide residue. And choose fresh. Avoid produce that is wilted, slimy, limp, overly soft, or turning brown. Some fruits and vegetables last longer than others. Dense produce can

Me as a little girl, hiding amidst the green beans and morning glories.

be bought in greater bulk, since it will last longer. This includes apples, carrots, and sweet potatoes. Of the greens, kale tends to last the longest. Frozen produce is also an acceptable alternative in many cases—produce frozen at its peak of ripeness maintains most of its nutrients. And I include canned tomatoes and corn in some recipes because it makes food preparation so much easier, and eating healthy is only going to happen for most of us if it doesn't require too many hours of our precious time.

Meat and Fish

You won't find a great abundance of meat recipes in this cookbook for a few reasons. Meat and fish are expensive compared to grains and produce; it can be difficult to source ethically raised, nutritionally sound meat; and I don't particularly like preparing it. I am not a vegetarian. Interestingly, I find that I'm able to digest meat better than I can many fruits, vegetables, and grains (though I know other people who have the exact oppositve experience). Also, I like meat. But I eat it in moderation and I try to get meat that is organic to avoid the hormones and antibiotics found in most commercially raised meat. When possible, I like to get meat from the local food co-op or from farmers who I know raise their animals in healthy environments. For fish, wild-caught salmon is one of the healthiest and most sustainable choices. If buying white fish, avoid grouper and monkfish, the first because of high mercury levels and the latter because they are being depleted. Pacific halibut is a good choice for a white fish.

Sweeteners

Honey and maple syrup are great for use in a range of desserts and baked goods. They don't caramelize the way cane sugar does, but unless you're making hard candy or taffy, caramelization isn't really necessary. Honey and maple syrup will raise your blood sugar, so if you're diabetic, these natural sugars are not a safe alternative to cane sugar for you. However, they are less refined than granulated cane sugar and have some health benefits—especially honey.

HONEY
The best honey—both for nutrition and flavor—is in its raw form. Raw honey is a powerful antioxidant and has antiviral, antibacterial, and antifungal properties. It strengthens the immune system and can fight allergies (particularly if the honey is from local bees).

MAPLE SYRUP
Maple syrup is, well, delicious. I'm from Vermont, so I grew up tapping trees and boiling down the sap to make our liquid gold. Maple syrup doesn't rank quite as high as honey on the health scorecard, but it does have a lot of anti-inflammatory and antioxidant properties. Be sure to use 100% real maple syrup, not a syrup that's artificially flavored.

WHAT ABOUT AGAVE?
Agave, sometimes called "the great Mexican aloe," produces a sweet sap, or nectar, that is traditionally extracted from the leaves, filtered, and heated to become a concentrated syrup—sort of like the tropical version of maple syrup. However, most agave sweeteners you can find in stores come from the blue agave plant, and rather than the sap being extracted from the leaves, it comes from the starchy root bulb. The agave glucose is converted to syrup through an enzymatic and chemical process that is similar to how cornstarch is converted to high fructose corn syrup (HFCS). And in case you missed the memo, HFCS messes with your hormones and makes you fat. I'm not a doctor, but unless you're going to go pick an agave leaf and extract the sap yourself, I'd stay away from it.

Fats
BUTTER VS. COCONUT OIL
Fats in general get a bad rap, but as you've probably heard by now, not all fats are created equal. Butter and coconut oil are both saturated fats. What that

means for health is a bit controversial. Recent studies have suggested that the correlation between saturated fats and heart disease may not be as direct as has been commonly thought for the last couple decades. Personally, I use butter in moderate amounts in my cooking and baking because it makes food delicious, it's high in Vitamins A, E, and K, and I find that eating a little butter helps me control sugar and carb cravings. I try to buy organic butter that's free of added hormones and antibiotics. Please do not substitute butter with margarine or other trans-fats-laden spreads—you won't be doing your health or your taste buds any favors.

I've also fallen in love with coconut oil. Coconuts are the latest darling of the health-conscious culinary crowd. And for good reasons! The saturated fat in coconut oil is made up of Medium Chain Triglycerides (MCTs), or fatty acids that are medium length. These MCTs are easily broken down by the digestive system and are sent directly to the liver, giving you quick energy. (For those of us choosing a gluten-free diet because of compromised digestive systems, any food that is easily digested is a cause for celebration!) The lauric acid in coconut oil boosts immunity, helping to kill off bad bacteria, viruses, and fungi. And I happen to love the just barely sweet flavor it contributes to cooking and baking. Look for organic, virgin coconut oil.

Butter and coconut oil behave very similarly in most recipes, so in many cases I've noted that you can use either. If you're dairy-intolerant, of course, opt for coconut oil.

OLIVE OIL
Populations that consume olive oil on a regular basis (mainly Mediterraneans) have been shown to have lower risk of cardiovascular issues, including heart disease, high blood pressure, and stroke. Olive oil is an anti-inflammatory and may even lessen depression and reduce the risk of breast cancer and Alzheimer's, and reduce oxidative stress in the liver. Look for extra virgin olive oil.

Starches and Gums
XANTHAN GUM
Xanthan gum is made by fermenting a sugar—usually corn sugar—with a bacteria called xanthomonas. It sounds scary, but from what I can tell it's harmless health-wise and does an impressive job of holding baked goods together in the absence of gluten. It's rather expensive, unfortunately, but you only ever use a tiny bit—I've never used more than a teaspoon in any baked good. Bob's Red Mill is the most common brand you'll see and is available in many supermarkets or online. Note that I don't include xanthan gum in my all-purpose flour mix (page 3). If the all-purpose mix you use does include xanthan gum, no need to add more xanthan gum to the recipes.

POTATO STARCH AND TAPIOCA STARCH
Potato starch and tapioca starch are both gluten-free and help to give your baked goods a nice consistency. They tend to be inexpensive compared to gluten-free flours and so are used in abundance in commercially produced gluten-free products. Since they have very little nutritional value I try to use them sparingly, but potato starch does make up ⅓ of my standard all-purpose gluten-free flour mix. Potato starch is lighter than tapioca starch and will make a fluffier, tender, springy bread product. Note that potato starch is not the same thing as potato flour and the two can't be used interchangeably.

Herbs and Spices
Using a variety of herbs and spices in your foods will add more than exciting flavors—most herbs and spices have powerful healing properties. Many are anti-inflammatories, which is good news because inflammation has been linked to many diseases and conditions, including arthritis, diabetes, high blood pressure, asthma, acne, Alzheimer's, and more. Many herbs and spices also aid in digestion, and others serve as natural antibiotics. On the next page I list some of the ones used most often in my recipes and their healing properties.

COMMON HEALING HERBS AND THEIR PROPERTIES

SPICE	HEALTH BENEFITS
Basil	Basil has powerful antibacterial and antiviral properties. It's also an anti-inflammatory and a good source of Vitamin A. It's sometimes used to treat constipation and indigestion. Try to have a tablespoon of fresh basil leaves or ½ teaspoon dried basil three times a week.
Cinnamon	Cinnamon has a number of antioxidant properties. It also helps to regulate insulin, which regulates blood sugar. It may also inhibit the formation of amyloid plaques in the brain, reducing the risk of Alzheimer's. Aim to have ¼ to ½ teaspoon ground cinnamon daily.
Cumin	Cumin helps to stimulate the production of pancreatic enzymes, which aid digestion. It's also a powerful antioxidant and anti-inflammatory, helps regulate insulin, and has anti-asthmatic properties.
Garlic	Garlic has powerful antibacterial, antifungal, and antimicrobial properties—it's often used to fight infections, especially ear infections. It also helps to lower LDL cholesterol, protecting against heart disease, and is a pain reducer. Use fresh garlic rather than dried or powdered.
Ginger	Ginger helps soothe nausea and stomach upset. It's also an anti-inflammatory and a pain reducer. Fresh ginger root is more effective than ground ginger.
Rosemary	Rosemary contains carnosol and rosemarinic acid, powerful antioxidants that counteract the cancer-causing effects of carcinogens. Use rosemary when frying, grilling, or broiling meats.
Turmeric	Turmeric is a spice that's used regularly in Ayurvedic medicine. It's a strong antioxidant that wards off cancer growth and Alzheimer's, among other things. It has anti-inflammatory properties, strengthens the immune system, and helps regulate insulin. Aim to have a teaspoon of ground turmeric at least three times a week. Fresh turmeric root is more effective than ground turmeric, but may be difficult to find.

The Healthy
GLUTEN-FREE
Diet

BREAKFAST AND BREADS

All-Purpose Gluten-Free Flour Mix

Makes 6 cups.

Ingredients

2 cups brown rice flour or
   brown sweet rice flour
2 cups sorghum flour
2 cups potato starch,
   tapioca starch, or
   arrowroot powder
   (choose two types of
   starch to combine for
   best results)

Mix the flours together and store in an airtight bag or canister in the refrigerator or freezer.

Sorghum flour is high in protein and fiber and has a lovely slight sweetness to it. I love it in baked goods, but for a slightly grainier texture you can also experiment with replacing the sorghum in this all-purpose mix with buckwheat, quinoa, millet, or teff flour. Almond and coconut flours are delicious but require more liquid and eggs in your recipe, so I wouldn't use them in an all-purpose mix.

Note that potato stach is not the same thing as potato flour; be sure to get the starch. However, tapioca flour and tapioca starch *are* the same thing.

Buckwheat Apple Pancakes

Makes about 12 medium pancakes.

Ingredients

¾ cup buckwheat flour

¾ cup all-purpose gluten-
free flour (page 3)

2 tablespoons brown sugar

¼ teaspoon salt

1 teaspoon baking soda

¼ teaspoon cinnamon

3 tablespoons butter or
coconut oil, melted

1 egg, lightly beaten

2 cups buttermilk

2 apples, peeled, cored,
and chopped in small
pieces

Butter, coconut oil, or
vegetable oil for the pan

Whisk together the dry ingredients and then pour the melted butter or oil over top and mix. Mix together the egg and buttermilk and add to the dry ingredients. Stir in the apple pieces just until incorporated—don't overmix.

Heat a griddle or frying pan and add enough butter or oil to lightly coat the surface. Have a plate nearby on which to place the pancakes when they're done (or you can put the oven on its lowest setting and place an oven-safe plate or pan inside to keep the pancakes warm until it's time to serve).

Ladle about ¼ cup of batter onto hot pan. If pan is big enough, you can do more than one pancake at once, as long as the edges don't touch. If they do run together, just use your spatula to cut them apart after they begin to firm up. Cook 2–3 minutes on the first side, or until bubbles begin to show on the top of the pancakes and they're firm enough to flip. Cook another 1–2 minutes on the other side until pancakes are lightly browned.

Continue until all batter is used, adding oil to the pan as necessary. Serve with butter and real maple syrup.

If you don't have buttermilk on hand, mix 2 cups of milk with 2 teaspoons of vinegar and allow to sit for a few minutes before using. Also, you can substitute the apples for berries or sliced bananas, or use a combination.

Sweet Potato Pancakes

Makes about 12 medium pancakes.

Ingredients

2 large sweet potatoes
(about 1¼ cups mashed)
1½ cups all-purpose
gluten-free flour (page 3)
3 teaspoons baking
powder
½ teaspoon salt
½ teaspoon cinnamon
¼ cup butter or coconut
oil, melted
2 eggs, beaten
1½ cups milk (dairy,
almond, soy, or coconut)
Butter, coconut oil, or
vegetable oil for the pan

Heat a pan of water to boiling. Peel and chop the sweet potatoes into 1" chunks. Boil for about 6 minutes or until soft when pricked with a fork. Drain and mash.

Whisk together the dry ingredients and then pour the melted butter or oil over top and mix. Mix together the egg, milk, and mashed sweet potatoes and add to the dry ingredients. Stir just until incorporated—don't overmix.

Heat a griddle or frying pan and add enough butter or oil to lightly coat the surface. Have a plate nearby on which to place the pancakes when they're done (or you can put the oven on its lowest setting and place an oven-safe plate or pan inside to keep the pancakes warm until it's time to serve).

Ladle about ¼ cup of batter onto hot pan. If pan is big enough, you can do more than one pancake at once, as long as the edges don't touch. If they do run together, just use your spatula to cut them apart after they begin to firm up. Cook 2–3 minutes on the first side, or until bubbles begin to show on the top of the pancakes and they're firm enough to flip. Cook another 1–2 minutes on the other side until pancakes are lightly browned.

Continue until all batter is used, adding oil to the pan as necessary. Serve with butter and real maple syrup.

Almond Flour Waffles

Makes 4 large squares.

Ingredients

3 eggs, separated
¼ cup milk (coconut, dairy, almond, or soy)
1 teaspoon vanilla
1 tablespoon maple syrup or honey
¼ cup butter or coconut oil, melted
1 cup almond flour
¼ teaspoon baking soda
¼ teaspoon salt

Turn on the waffle iron to heat.

Beat together the egg yolks and milk and add the vanilla, maple syrup, and melted butter or coconut oil. In a separate bowl, whisk or beat the egg whites until light and fluffy.

Whisk together the dry ingredients. Add the egg mixture and stir just until combined. Fold in the egg whites.

Grease waffle iron and cook according to the waffle iron instructions. For a standard waffle iron, pour about ¼ cup batter into the center of the iron, close the lid, and cook until lightly browned. Serve with maple syrup, apple compote (page 9), or fresh fruit and yogurt.

Apple Compote

Makes about 2 cups.

Ingredients

3 cups peeled and sliced
   apples
2 tablespoons butter
2 tablespoons brown sugar
½ teaspoon cinnamon

In a frying pan or cast-iron skillet, melt butter over medium heat. Add all ingredients and sauté for about 5 minutes or until apples are tender.

Almond Flour Banana Bread

Makes 1 loaf.

Ingredients

1½ cups all-purpose
   gluten-free flour (page 3)
1½ cups almond flour
1 teaspoon baking soda
½ teaspoon baking
   powder
½ teaspoon salt
3 eggs
2–3 very ripe bananas,
   mashed
⅓ cup brown sugar, honey,
   or maple syrup
¼ cup butter or coconut
   oil, softened
1 teaspoon vanilla extract
1 cup chocolate chips,
   raisins, or walnuts
   (optional)

Preheat oven to 350°F and grease a loaf pan. In a large mixing bowl, whisk together all dry ingredients.

In a separate bowl, mix together the wet ingredients. Fold the wet ingredients into the dry and mix to incorporate. Mix in chocolate chips, raisins, or walnuts if using.

Pour into the bread pan and bake 35–40 minutes or until a toothpick inserted into the center comes out fairly clean. Allow to cool until pan can be handled and then remove from pan and continue cooling on a wire rack.

You can use all almond flour in this recipe instead of the 1½ cups of all-purpose gluten-free flour. Using all almond flour will yield a somewhat denser (and more expensive) loaf.

Hot Amaranth Cereal

Makes 2 servings.

Ingredients

½ cup amaranth
1 cup water
¼ teaspoon salt
1 cup milk (coconut, dairy, almond, or soy)
2 tablespoons honey or maple syrup
½ teaspoon vanilla
½ teaspoon cinnamon
Fresh berries or other fruit and/or nuts

Combine the amaranth, water, and salt in a medium saucepan and bring to a boil. Reduce heat to low and simmer for about 20 minutes or until the water is mostly absorbed. The amaranth grains should still look distinct—not like a pile of mush.

Stir in the remaining ingredients and serve warm.

Amaranth is very high in fiber, protein, calcium, iron, and magnesium. This cereal can be cooked the day before and refrigerated—in the morning, simply reheat and stir in the milk, sweetener, spices, and other desired toppings.

Oatmeal Pumpkin Muffins

Makes 12 muffins.

Ingredients

1½ cups all-purpose
   gluten-free flour (page 3)
1½ cups gluten-free old-
   fashioned oats
½ cup brown sugar or
   ⅓ cup maple syrup or
   honey
1 teaspoon baking powder
½ teaspoon baking soda
½ teaspoon salt
1 teaspoon cinnamon
1 teaspoon ground ginger
1½ cups pumpkin purée
3 tablespoons olive oil or
   melted coconut oil
¼ cup milk (dairy, almond,
   coconut, or soy)
2 teaspoons vanilla extract
2 eggs, lightly beaten
½ cup dark chocolate
   chips, raisins, cranberries,
   or peeled, chopped
   apple (optional)

Preheat oven to 375°F. Grease a 12-cup muffin tin or line with cupcake liners.

Whisk together all the dry ingredients. In a separate bowl, whisk together the pumpkin, oil, milk, vanilla, and eggs and add to the dry ingredients, mixing until incorporated. Add the chocolate chips, raisins, cranberries, or chopped apples and stir just until evenly distributed.

Fill muffin tins nearly full and bake for about 20 minutes or until a toothpick inserted into the center of a muffin comes out fairly clean.

Berry Lemon Chia Muffins

Makes about a dozen muffins.

Ingredients

½ cup coconut flour
3 tablespoons chia seeds
¼ teaspoon baking soda
⅛ teaspoon salt
½ cup milk (dairy, almond,
  coconut, or soy)
½ cup honey or maple
  syrup
4 eggs
½ cup butter or coconut
  oil, melted
½ teaspoon vanilla extract
1 lemon, juice and zest
1 cup berries, any kind
  (fresh or frozen)

Preheat oven to 350°F and grease a muffin tin.

In a medium mixing bowl, whisk together the dry ingredients. In a separate large bowl, whisk together the milk, honey or maple syrup, eggs, melted butter or coconut oil, and vanilla extract.

Add the dry mixture to the wet, stirring to incorporate. Add the lemon juice and zest and blueberries and stir until combined.

Fill muffin cups about ¾ full and bake about 20 minutes or until a toothpick inserted into the center comes out relatively clean.

Coconut flour makes these muffins moist, chewy, and delicious. The muffins may not rise as much as the fluffy muffins you see in bakeries and delis, but they're nutritious and delicious.

Baked Frittata

Makes 6 servings.

Ingredients

Olive oil for pan
1 small onion, finely
  chopped
½ cup finely chopped
  mushrooms (any variety)
1½ cups chopped fresh
  spinach
8 eggs
½ cup Greek-style yogurt
1 teaspoon salt
½ teaspoon black pepper
½ cup fresh chopped
  herbs, such as parsley,
  dill, cilantro, or tarragon
  or 3–4 tablespoons dried
  (optional)
¾ cup freshly grated
  cheddar cheese
  (optional)

Preheat oven to 400°F. Heat a 10" cast-iron skillet on the stovetop over medium heat. Coat bottom of pan with olive oil.

Sauté onions and mushrooms about five minutes or until onions are translucent. Add the spinach and herbs (if using) and sauté another few minutes to wilt the spinach. In a small bowl, beat together the eggs, yogurt, salt, and pepper. Reduce heat to low and pour the egg mixture over the top of the veggies. Cook uncovered, without stirring, for about five minutes. Sprinkle grated cheese over the top, if using.

Turn off stovetop unit and transfer pan to the oven. Bake uncovered for another 3–5 minutes or until egg is set and cheese is slightly browned. Do not overcook. Slice and serve.

Pumpkin Cornbread

Makes 12 servings.

Ingredients

1 cup all-purpose gluten-free flour (page 3)
1 cup cornmeal (preferably organic)
1 tablespoon baking powder
1 teaspoon salt
½ teaspoon cinnamon
⅓ cup brown sugar or honey
2 eggs
1 cup pumpkin purée
¼ cup olive oil or coconut oil, melted
1 tablespoon molasses

Preheat oven to 400°F and grease an 8" x 8" baking pan.

In a medium mixing bowl, whisk together the dry ingredients. In a separate bowl, combine all remaining ingredients, mixing until well combined. Pour the wet ingredients into the dry and stir just until combined.

Pour into the prepared pan and bake about 25 minutes or until a toothpick inserted into the center comes out mostly clean.

Sweet Potato Scones

Makes a dozen scones.

1 medium sweet potato
(about 1 cup mashed)
1½ cups all-purpose
gluten-free flour
¾ cup oat flour
¼ cup brown sugar
2 teaspoons baking
powder
½ teaspoon xanthan gum
¼ teaspoon salt
1 teaspoon cinnamon
6 tablespoons butter or
coconut oil, cold
1 egg
4 tablespoons cold milk
1 teaspoon vanilla

Preheat oven to 425°F and grease a baking sheet. Heat a pan of water to boiling. Peel and chop the sweet potato into 1" chunks. Boil for about 6 minutes or until soft when pricked with a fork. Drain, mash, and place in refrigerator to chill.

Whisk together flours, brown sugar, baking powder, xanthan gum, salt, and cinnamon. Cut the butter or oil into the flour mixture and use your fingers to incorporate until the mixture resembles coarse crumbs.

In a small bowl, whisk together the egg, milk, and vanilla. Pour into the flour mixture, add mashed sweet potato, and stir to combine.

Turn the dough onto a lightly floured surface, divide into two balls, and knead each 7 or 8 times. Place dough balls on cookie sheet and flatten each into circles that are about ¾" thick. Slice into sixths but don't separate the wedges. Bake for about 20 minutes or until tops and edges begin to brown. Dough will still be moist in the center. Remove from oven, use a spatula to separate the wedges, and cool on racks. Store in an airtight container in the refrigerator or freezer.

Keeping all the ingredients cold while preparing the dough will result in flakier scones. Scones are best served warm and are delicious with jam.

Yogurt Parfait

Makes 4 servings.

Ingredients

2 cups vanilla yogurt (page 21)

½ pint fresh strawberries, washed, hulled, and sliced

½ pint fresh blueberries

½ cup gluten-free granola (page 23) or toasted slivered almonds

Place a spoonful of yogurt in the bottom of each of four mini parfait glasses. Place a layer of strawberries on top, then more yogurt. Add a layer of blueberries, and then top it off with more yogurt. Sprinkle granola or nuts over the top just before serving.

Homemade Crockpot Yogurt

Makes about 4 cups of yogurt.

Ingredients

1 quart milk, preferably organic

1 tablespoon plain yogurt with live active cultures

1 tablespoon honey or maple syrup (optional)

2 teaspoons vanilla extract (optional)

Equipment

Crockpot

Candy thermometer

Towels

Pour the milk into the crockpot and turn heat on to medium-high. Add honey or maple syrup if using. Cover pot and allow milk to heat for about 30 minutes and then use the candy thermometer to take the temperature. The goal is to reach 180°F. If you're not there yet, return lid to pot and continue to heat. When milk reaches 180°F, turn off the slow cooker, remove lid, and allow milk to cool to 120°F (about 30 minutes).

While milk is cooling, place one tablespoon yogurt in a bowl and allow to warm to room temperature. When milk is at 120°F, add the yogurt to the milk, stir gently until yogurt dissolves, place the lid on the pot, and wrap thick towels around the outside of the pot to insulate it. Place in a safe place where it won't be moved or shaken for 6–8 hours or overnight. Then move to refrigerator to continue setting for about 4 hours or until desired thickness is reached.

Add vanilla or other flavoring if desired and stir. Store covered in the refrigerator for 10–20 days.

Granola

Makes 4 cups.

Ingredients

3 cups gluten-free old-
  fashioned oats
½ cup sliced almonds
¼ cup butter or coconut
  oil
2 tablespoons honey
2 tablespoons brown sugar
1 teaspoon cinnamon
1 teaspoon vanilla
½ cup dried cherries or
  cranberries, or raisins

Heat oven to 325°F. In a medium-sized mixing bowl, stir together the oats and sliced almonds.

In a saucepan over low heat, stir together the butter or coconut oil, honey, brown sugar, and cinnamon until melted and combined. Remove from heat, add vanilla, and stir. Pour over oats and mix thoroughly.

Line a baking sheet with parchment paper or foil. Spread granola mixture evenly over the pan and bake for 20–25 minutes, stirring granola with a spatula once or twice part-way through.

Remove from oven and fold in dried fruit. Allow to cool completely before storing in an airtight container.

Cherry Clafoutis

Makes 12 clafoutis.

Ingredients

4 eggs
¾ cup sugar
2 teaspoons lemon zest
1 teaspoon vanilla
1 cup milk (dairy, coconut, soy, or almond)
¾ cup all-purpose gluten-free flour (page 3) or almond flour
¼ teaspoon salt
1 cup halved and pitted cherries
Confectioners' sugar, for dusting

Preheat oven to 325°F. Grease 12 muffin cups.

In a large mixing bowl, beat together eggs, sugar, lemon zest, and vanilla. Add milk and beat another 30 seconds or so. Stir in the flour and salt.

Fill each muffin cup about ¾ of the way, place 3 or 4 cherry halves on top of the batter in each cup, and bake for 20–25 minutes, or until a toothpick inserted in the middle of one comes out clean.

Just before serving, dust with confectioners' sugar.

Cheddar-Herb Drop Biscuits

Makes 20 biscuits.

Ingredients

2¼ cups all-purpose
   gluten-free flour (page 3)
1 tablespoon baking
   powder
½ teaspoon xanthan gum
¼ teaspoon salt
2 teaspoons sugar
½ cup cold unsalted butter
1⅓ cups buttermilk
1 cup grated cheddar
   cheese
1 tablespoon fresh
   rosemary, dill, or other
   favorite herb, coarsely
   chopped, or 1 teaspoon
   dried herbs.
1 teaspoon black pepper

Preheat oven to 450°F. In a large mixing bowl, whisk together flour, baking soda, baking powder, xanthan gum, salt, and sugar. Chop the butter into small pieces and use fingers or two forks to crumble it into the flour, mixing until butter is in pea-sized chunks. Add the cheddar, rosemary, and pepper and mix just slightly.

Add the buttermilk and stir just until combined. Drop onto a cookie sheet and bake about 15 minutes or until biscuits are lightly browned on top.

If you don't have buttermilk on hand, mix 2 cups of milk with 2 teaspoons of vinegar and allow to sit for a few minutes before using.

Oatmeal Bread

Makes one 10-inch loaf.

Ingredients

1½ teaspoons yeast

1¼ cups milk, room temperature

2 cups all-purpose gluten-free flour (page 3)

1 cup gluten-free oat flour

⅔ cup old-fashioned rolled oats

½ teaspoon salt

2 eggs

2 tablespoons butter or coconut oil, melted

3 tablespoons brown sugar or honey

¾ cup raisins (optional)

Add yeast to the milk and allow to sit while you prepare the rest of the dough.

In a medium bowl, combine flours, oats, and salt.

In a separate bowl, whisk together eggs, butter or oil, and brown sugar or honey. Pour into flour mixture, add milk and yeast, and stir to combine. Dough will be wet—not like typical bread dough that you could knead.

Grease a bread pan thoroughly. Pour batter into pan, cover with a light towel, and set in a warm place for about 45 minutes.

Heat the oven to 350°F. Bake for about 45 minutes or until top is lightly golden. Remove from pan, transfer to a cooling rack, and allow to cool most of the way before cutting. When fully cool, store in an airtight bag in the refrigerator or slice and freeze.

You can easily make oat flour in a food processor fitted with a steel blade. Just process the oats until they become flour.

ENTREES

Polenta Feta Shrimp Bake

Makes 4 servings.

Ingredients

1 tablespoon olive oil
2 cloves garlic, peeled and
minced
Small red onion, peeled
and diced
2 tubes polenta
1 jar spaghetti sauce
3 spicy sausages, sliced
1 pound shrimp, cooked,
peeled, and deveined
⅔ cup crumbled feta
cheese

Preheat oven to 425°F.

Heat the olive oil in a sauté pan. Add the garlic and onions and sauté until soft, about 3 minutes. Add the sliced sausages and cook until lightly browned. Remove from heat.

Slice one tube of polenta into ¼"–½" pieces and arrange to make a single layer on the bottom of an 8" x 8" casserole dish. Cover with a thin layer of spaghetti sauce and then sprinkle half of the garlic, onion, and sausage over the top, followed by half of the shrimp. Sprinkle ⅓ cup crumbled feta evenly over the top. Repeat to create another layer of all ingredients, starting with the polenta slices and ending with the feta.

Bake until the cheese is melted on top and the shrimp is hot, about 12 minutes.

Maple Citrus-Glazed Salmon

Makes 4 servings.

Ingredients

1 salmon fillet (about 1½ pounds), preferably wild Alaskan

3 tablespoons maple syrup

3 tablespoons balsamic vinegar

1 tablespoon orange juice

⅛ teaspoon kosher salt

⅛ teaspoon freshly ground black pepper

Heat oven to 450°F. Line a baking sheet with parchment paper and place salmon, skin side down, on top.

In a small bowl, whisk together the maple syrup, balsamic vinegar, orange juice, and salt and pepper. Brush half of the glaze over the salmon.

Bake for 10 minutes, brush with remaining glaze, and bake about 5 minutes more or until fish flakes easily with fork.

Salmon is full of omega-3 oils, which help to reduce bad cholesterol and inflammation. Farm-raised salmon are often fed antibiotics and are high in mercury, so try to buy wild Alaskan salmon instead.

Quinoa Risotto with Shitake Mushrooms and Arugula

Makes 4 servings.

Ingredients

1 tablespoons olive oil
½ yellow onion, peeled and chopped
1 clove garlic, peeled and minced
½ cup shitake mushrooms, thinly sliced
1 cup quinoa, uncooked
¼ cup white wine
2¼ cups chicken or vegetable broth
2 cups arugula
½ cup grated Parmesan cheese (optional)
Salt and pepper to taste
Fresh thyme, minced (for garnish)

Rinse the quinoa in a fine-mesh strainer.

Place a large saucepan over medium heat and add the olive oil. Add the onion and sauté until soft, about 5 minutes. Add the garlic and mushrooms and sauté another three minutes.

Add the quinoa and cook, stirring, for two minutes. Pour in the white wine and simmer until the liquid is absorbed. Add ½ cup of the chicken or vegetable broth and allow to boil. Reduce heat to low and simmer, stirring occasionally, until the liquid is absorbed. Continue adding ½ cup at a time, stirring and allowing the liquid to be absorbed between each addition. Once all the liquid is absorbed and the quinoa is tender, toss in the arugula and cook until wilted.

Fold in the Parmesan, if using. Add salt and pepper to taste and garnish with fresh thyme.

Risotto is typically made with arborio rice, which is gluten-free and delicious but doesn't have a lot of nutritional value. Quinoa is high in protein and fiber and other nutrients and is similar to Arborio rice in its ability to absorb flavors.

Soba Noodle Stir-Fry

Makes 4 servings.

Ingredients

12 ounces (1 package) soba noodles

4 teaspoons sesame oil, divided

2 cloves garlic, peeled and minced

2 teaspoons minced ginger

8 heads baby bok choy, washed and sliced into strips

2 medium carrots, coarsely grated

4 tablespoons rice vinegar

3 tablespoons gluten-free tamari

1 tablespoon maple syrup

½ teaspoon red pepper flakes

Small handful fresh mint

Salt to taste

Boil a pot of water and cook the soba noodles according to instructions. Drain and set aside.

While the soba noodles are cooking, heat 2 tablespoons of sesame oil in a large wok or sauté pan. Saute the minced garlic and ginger for 2 to 3 minutes. Add the carrots and bok choy and sauté for another few minutes, until carrots begin to soften.

In a small bowl, whisk together the remaining 2 teaspoons sesame oil, rice vinegar, tamari, maple syrup, and red pepper flakes. Pour over vegetables. Add soba noodles and fresh mint and continue to sauté, stirring, for a few more minutes. Add salt to taste. Serve hot or chilled.

Vegetarian Chili

Makes 6 servings.

Ingredients

1 tablespoon olive oil
1 medium onion, peeled and chopped
2 cloves garlic, peeled and minced
1 bell pepper (any color), chopped
1 jalapeno, seeds removed, diced (optional)
3 (15-ounce) cans diced tomatoes, with liquid
2 (15-ounce) cans red kidney beans, with liquid
2 (15-ounce) cans black beans, with liquid
1 (15-ounce) can corn, with liquid
2 tablespoons cumin
1 tablespoon chili powder
Salt and pepper to taste

Heat oil in a large saucepan or Dutch oven over medium heat. Sauté the onion and garlic until onions are tender, about 5 minutes. Add the bell pepper and sauté another 5 minutes.

Add remaining ingredients, stir, and simmer for at least 20 minutes, stirring occasionally. Add salt and pepper to taste.

Serve with sour cream and shredded cheese, if desired. Delicious served with cornbread (see page 16).

Chicken Pad Thai

Makes 4–6 servings

Ingredients

2 cloves garlic, peeled
3" fresh ginger root, peeled
1 cup smooth peanut butter
¼ cup gluten-free tamari
2 tablespoons rice vinegar (or substitute with balsamic vinegar)
1 tablespoon lime juice (about ½ lime)
2 tablespoons brown sugar
¼ teaspoon cayenne pepper
½ cup water
½ pound rice noodles
1 tablespoon olive oil
1 pound boneless, skinless chicken breast
1 medium carrot, cut in long, thin strips
2 eggs
2 cups bean sprouts
⅓ cup dry-roasted unsalted peanuts, crushed
3 scallions, sliced (greens and whites)
½ lime, cut into wedges

Sauce can be made up to a week ahead and refrigerated until use. To make, drop the peeled garlic and ginger into the mouth of a food processor and process until finely chopped. Add remaining ingredients and process until smooth. If you don't have a food processor, mince the garlic and ginger and then stir all ingredients together in a medium bowl.

Bring a large pot of water to a boil. Drop in noodles, stir to separate them, and turn off the heat. Allow the noodles to soak in the hot water for 5–6 minutes, or until flexible but not fully softened. Drain and rinse quickly in cold water.

Cut chicken into 1" pieces. Place a large wok or frying pan over medium heat and add 1 tablespoon olive oil, swirling to coat the pan. Sauté the chicken until just cooked through, about 4 minutes. Drain off the juices and return to heat.

Add the carrots and sauté for about a minute. Push contents of the pan to the side and crack in the two eggs in the space you made, stirring quickly to scramble.

Dump the noodles into the pan and add a few tablespoons of the sauce. Stir to separate noodles and mix contents of pan (it helps to use two large forks). Add more sauce, a few tablespoons at a time, continuing to stir until all sauce is used and noodles are tender. Stir in 1 cup of the bean sprouts.

Scoop pad Thai into a serving dish and garnish with the remaining bean sprouts, crushed peanuts, sliced scallions, and lime wedges.

Grass-Fed Steak Salad with Ginger-Balsamic Dressing

Makes 4 servings.

Ingredients

1 pound grass-fed rib-eye, strip steak, or skirt steak, extra fat trimmed

Marinade/Dressing
2" fresh ginger root, peeled
1 garlic clove, peeled
¼ cup balsamic vinegar
2 tablespoons gluten-free tamari
2 tablespoons lime juice
1 cup olive oil
½ teaspoon kosher salt
½ teaspoon black pepper

Salad
½ pound leafy greens (romaine, arugula, raddiccio, etc.)
1 pint cherry or grape tomatoes
½ cup crumbled blue cheese (optional)

Drop the ginger root and garlic clove in the mouth of a food processor and process until minced. Add the balsamic vinegar, tamari, and lime juice, and mix. With the food processor running, slowly drizzle the olive oil into the mouth of the food processor in a very thin stream. Add the salt and pepper.

Place the steak in a sealable plastic bag and pour in half of the marinade. Refrigerate for about 2 hours.

Grill or sauté the steak over medium-high heat about 2 minutes on each side, or until desired doneness. Transfer to a cutting board and cut on a diagonal into thin slices.

Rinse the salad greens, pat or spin dry, and place in a salad bowl. Add the tomatoes and blue cheese and toss with desired amount of remaining dressing. Arrange the steak on top and serve.

Quinoa-Stuffed Acorn Squash

Makes 2 servings.

Ingredients

1 acorn squash, halved and seeded
1 cup quinoa, uncooked
2 cups chicken or vegetable broth
2 tablespoons olive oil, divided
¼ red onion, peeled and diced (about ¼ cup)
3 cups kale, rinsed and broken into small pieces
1 tablespoon maple syrup
¼ teaspoon kosher salt
⅛ teaspoon black pepper
⅛ teaspoon cinnamon
¼ cup dried cranberries
3 tablespoons grated Parmesan

Heat the oven to 400°F. Brush the insides of the acorn squash halves with olive oil and place them face down on a baking sheet. Bake for 20–25 minutes or until soft.

Place the quinoa and broth in a saucepan and simmer, covered, for about 12 minutes, or until all liquid is absorbed. Add the maple syrup, salt, pepper, and cinnamon and mix. Add the cranberries.

Place a frying pan over medium heat and add oil to coat the pan. Sauté the onion until soft. Add the kale and sauté until wilted.

Mix together the quinoa mixture with the kale mixture and scoop into the squash hollows. Sprinkle with Parmesan and serve.

Fish Tacos

Makes 2 servings (4 tacos).

Ingredients
4 small corn tortillas
½ pound white fish, such
  as cod or red snapper
  fillets, cut into about
  1" x 4" strips
1 tablespoon olive oil
1 teaspoon cumin
1 tablespoon lime juice

Cole Slaw
1 cup shredded cabbage
2 teaspoons olive oil
⅛ teaspoon kosher salt
1 teaspoon lime juice

Guacamole
½ avocado
2 tablespoons Greek
  yogurt
1 teaspoon chopped fresh
  cilantro
1 tablespoon lime juice
⅛ teaspoon kosher salt

In a medium frying pan, combine the olive oil, cumin, and lime juice. Place the fish strips in the mixture and toss to coat. Cook over medium-high heat, stirring constantly, for about 5 minutes or until fish flakes easily with a fork.

In a medium-sized mixing bowl combine all ingredients for cole slaw.

In a separate bowl, mash the avocado with the Greek yogurt. Add the cilantro, lime juice, and salt, and mix.

If desired, heat tortillas in a frying pan or in the micro-wave. Place a dollop of guacamole in the center of each taco and then divide the fish between the four tortillas. Top with the cole slaw and serve.

Layered Spinach Enchiladas

Makes 4 servings.

Ingredients

1 tablespoon olive oil
½ onion, peeled and
  chopped
10 ounces fresh spinach
  leaves
1 (14-ounce) can diced
  tomatoes
3 teaspoons minced
  canned chipotle chilis
1½ cups Greek-style
  yogurt
8 (6") corn tortillas
1½ cups shredded
  Monterey Jack cheese

Heat oven to 450°F. In a large saucepan, heat the olive oil over medium heat. Add the onion and sauté until translucent. Add the spinach and cook, stirring, until wilted. Add the diced tomatoes, chipotle chilis, and yogurt and simmer until bubbly.

Grease an 8" x 8" baking dish. Smear ¼ cup of the spinach mixture on the bottom of the pan, followed by four tortillas, overlapping. Cover with the rest of the sauce, followed by the remaining tortillas. Sprinkle the cheese on top and bake for about 25 minutes or until cheese is bubbly and golden. To serve, cut into squares and lift out with a spatula.

Quinoa Taboulleh

Makes 6 servings.

Ingredients

1 cup quinoa, rinsed
½ teaspoon kosher salt
1½ cups frozen peas
2 tablespoons butter or
   coconut oil
½ cup chopped fresh mint
4 tablespoons goat cheese
½ teaspoon lemon zest

Combine quinoa, kosher, salt, and 1¼ cups water in a saucepan over high heat and bring to a boil. Reduce heat, cover, and simmer for about 10 minutes, or until quinoa is soft. Remove from heat and allow to rest, covered, for another 5 minutes.

While quinoa is resting, boil 2 cups of water in a saucepan, pour in the frozen peas, and cook over medium heat for about 4 minutes, or just until peas are hot. Do not overcook. Drain.

Fluff quinoa with a fork and add the butter or coconut oil, fresh mint, goat cheese, and lemon zest. Mix and then fold in the peas. Serve hot or cold. Season with more salt or black pepper if desired.

Coconut Curry

Makes 6 servings.

Ingredients

1 tablespoon olive oil
1 medium onion, peeled
   and sliced
2 cloves garlic, peeled and
   minced
1 teaspoon salt
1 teaspoon turmeric
½ teaspoon ground
   coriander
1 teaspoon ground cumin
⅛ teaspoon cloves
⅛ teaspoon cinnamon
¼ teaspoon cayenne
   pepper
1 tablespoon gluten-free
   tamari
1 tablespoon brown sugar
1 (14-ounce) can coconut
   milk
½ cup chicken or
   vegetable broth
1 tablespoon lime juice
2 medium potatoes, cut
   into chunks
1 (15-ounce) can chickpeas
Handful fresh basil
Steamed rice or quinoa,
   for serving

In a large sauté pan or wok, heat the oil. Add the chopped onion and minced garlic and sauté until onions are translucent. Add all the spices and sauté until fragrant.

Add the tamari, brown sugar, coconut milk, broth, lime juice, and potato chunks. Drain and rinse the chickpeas and add to mixture. Simmer until the potatoes are soft (about 8 minutes). Add the basil leaves, simmer for another 1–2 minutes, and serve with steamed rice or quinoa.

Shepherd's Pie

Makes 6 servings.

Ingredients

1 sweet potato
1 potato
1 tablespoon olive oil
½ red onion, peeled and chopped
1 lb ground beef
½ cup beef broth or water
10 ounces frozen mixed vegetables
⅛ teaspoon herbes de Provence
⅛ teaspoon marjoram
2 teaspoons milk, divided
1 tablespoon salted butter, divided
⅛ teaspoon salt
¼ cup shredded cheddar cheese

Heat two pots of water to a boil. Peel and chop the sweet potato and white potato and boil each in separate pots until soft (about 10 minutes). Drain.

Meanwhile, heat 1 tablespoon oil in a frying pan. Sauté the onions until soft. Add the ground beef and cook until brown. Add the broth or water, frozen vegetables, herbs, and salt. Cook, stirring, until vegetables are soft. Remove from heat. Heat oven to 375°F.

Mash the potato and sweet potato, adding 1 teaspoon milk, ½ tablespoon butter, and a dash of salt to each (⅛ teaspoon total).

Scoop the meat and vegetable mixture into a deep pie plate or casserole dish. Spread the mashed potato over the top, and then create a swirl pattern by dabbing the mashed sweet potato on top. Sprinkle with cheese.

Bake for about 20 minutes, or until cheese on top is melted and just beginning to turn golden.

Moroccan Chickpea Slow Cooker Stew

Makes 6 servings.

Ingredients

For Slow Cooker

2 medium sweet potatoes, washed and chopped (leave peels on)

1 pound butternut squash, peeled and chopped in bite-sized pieces

2 carrots, washed and cut in ½" pieces

1 medium yellow onion, peeled and diced

1 can chickpeas, drained and rinsed, or 2 cups soaked dried chickpeas

1 (14.5-ounce) can diced tomatoes with juices

2 cups chicken or vegetable broth

2 teaspoons cumin

1 teaspoon turmeric

½ teaspoon ground ginger

½ teaspoon ground cinnamon

½ teaspoon salt

¼ teaspoon black pepper

2 cloves garlic, peeled and minced

For Garnish (optional)

1 cup pitted green brined olives

Toasted slivered almonds

Plain yogurt

Steamed basmati rice or quinoa for serving

Place all ingredients (except for garnish ingredients and rice) in a slow cooker, stir, and cook at low heat for about 6 hours or until vegetables are tender.

Stir in green olives, if using. Serve over steamed rice or quinoa. Garnish with sliced almonds and a dollop of yogurt if desired.

Flatbread Pizza Crust

Makes one 10-inch pizza.

Ingredients

½ cup potato or tapioca
  starch
½ cup brown rice flour
½ cup milk (dairy, almond,
  or soy)
1 egg
1 teaspoon salt
1 teaspoon dried basil
1 teaspoon dried oregano

Preheat oven to 425°F.

In a medium-sized mixing bowl, stir together all ingredients. Batter will be runny.

Pour batter onto a well-greased baking sheet and spread gently with a spoon. Bake for 10 minutes. Remove from oven, add toppings, and bake an additional 10 minutes or until cheese is melted and slightly brown.

Spring Pizza

Makes one 10-inch pizza.

Ingredients

1 flatbread pizza crust
  (page 52)
1 cup sliced baby bella
  mushrooms
6 spears asparagus, ends
  trimmed and spears
  chopped into 1" pieces
½ cup chopped figs (fresh
  or dried)
4 ounces prosciutto
1 cup shredded mozzarella
3 tablespoons grated
  Romano cheese

Prepare the pizza crust according to instructions on page 52. Remove partially baked crust from oven and set aside.

Blanch the asparagus (cook in boiling water for about one minute, drain, and dunk quickly in ice water).

Arrange the mushrooms, blanched asparagus, and fig pieces on the crust. Tear the prosciutto into strips and distribute evenly over the pizza. Sprinkle the mozzarella over the top and bake at 425°F for about 10 minutes, or until the cheese is fully melted. Remove from oven, dust with Romano cheese, and serve.

Summer Pizza

Makes one 10-inch pizza.

Ingredients

1 flatbread pizza crust
(page 52)
3 tablespoons tomato
paste
½ teaspoon dried basil
¼ teaspoon salt
¼ cup fresh basil leaves
1 tomato, sliced
2 cups shredded
mozzarella
1 cup baby arugula
2 tablespoons balsamic
vinegar
2 tablespoons olive oil

Prepare the pizza crust according to instructions on page 52. Remove partially baked crust from oven and set aside.

Mix the tomato paste with the dried basil and salt and spread evenly over the partially baked crust. Arrange the tomato slices and fresh basil leaves on top and cover with shredded cheese. Bake for about 10 minutes, or until cheese is golden and bubbly.

Pile the fresh arugula on top of the pizza. Mix together the balsamic vinegar and olive oil and drizzle over the top. Serve immediately.

Fall Pizza

Makes one 10-inch pizza.

Ingredients

1 flatbread pizza crust
  (page 52)
1 cup shredded mozzarella
1½ cups butternut squash
  cubes
1 tablespoon olive oil
2 cups kale
2 ounces goat cheese

Prepare the pizza crust according to instructions on page 52. Remove partially baked crust from oven and set aside.

Heat a large pot of water to boiling. Add squash cubes and boil for about 10 minutes or until soft. Sauté the kale in a tablespoon of olive oil until it begins to wilt (about 3 minutes).

Spread the shredded mozzarella over the partially baked crust. Distribute the squash cubes evenly over the mozzarella, followed by the kale. Crumble the goat cheese over the top and bake at 425°F for another 10 minutes or until cheese begins to brown.

Winter Pizza

Makes one 10-inch pizza.

Ingredients

1 flatbread pizza crust
(page 52)
1 tablespoon olive oil
1 red onion, peeled and
sliced
1 teaspoon balsamic
vinegar
1 teaspoon thyme, fresh
and finely chopped, or ½
teaspoon dried
1 large potato, washed
and very thinly sliced
½ cup shredded cheddar
1 egg
Freshly ground salt and
pepper

Prepare the pizza crust according to instructions on page 52. Remove partially baked crust from oven and set aside.

Sauté the onion in the oil until it begins to brown. Transfer to the bowl of a food processor. Add balsamic vinegar and thyme and process until mixture forms a marmalade consistency. Spread evenly over pizza crust.

Arrange potato slices neatly over the surface of the pizza. Sprinkle the shredded cheese on top. Bake at 425°F for about 10 minutes, or until potato slices are soft. Remove from oven. Carefully crack an egg into a cup and then pour it onto the center of the pizza. Return to oven and bake another 10 minutes or until the egg white is set (yolk can still be slightly runny). Sprinkle with salt and pepper and serve immediately.

Pumpkin Curry

Makes 4 servings.

Ingredients

2 tablespoons olive or
coconut oil
1 tablespoon minced
ginger
1 tablespoon minced
garlic
1 cup quinoa, rinsed
3 cups chicken broth
1½ cups coconut milk
3 teaspoons curry powder
⅛ teaspoon cayenne
pepper
½ teaspoon salt
3 cups pumpkin or
butternut squash cubes
1 small tomato, chopped

In a medium saucepan, sauté the ginger, garlic, and raw quinoa in oil for about one minute. Add the chicken broth, coconut milk, curry powder, cayenne, salt, and pumpkin or butternut squash.

Simmer over medium-low heat for about 20 minutes, or until squash or pumpkin is just barely soft when pricked with a fork. Add tomato and cook another 5 minutes.

Spaghetti Squash with Sausage, Mushroom, and Spinach Sauce

Makes 4 servings.

Ingredients

1 medium spaghetti squash (about 3¼ pounds)
1 tablespoon olive oil
1 medium onion, peeled and chopped
2 cloves garlic, peeled and minced
12 ounces precooked chicken or turkey sausage links, chopped into small pieces
¾ pound baby bella or wild mushrooms, rinsed
2 (14.5-ounce) cans crushed tomatoes, undrained
1 tablespoon dried oregano
1 tablespoon dried basil
½ teaspoon crushed red pepper
1 teaspoon honey
Salt and pepper to taste
3 cups baby spinach leaves
Parmesan cheese (optional)

Preheat oven to 375°F. With a sharp knife, poke holes in the squash all over. Place on a baking sheet with a rim and roast about 1 hour and 20 minutes, or until a fork can easily be inserted into the squash. Remove from oven.

While the squash is baking, begin the sauce. Heat olive oil in a skillet over medium heat. Add the onion and sauté until soft. Add the garlic and sausage pieces and cook until the sausage just barely begins to brown. Add mushrooms and cook for another few minutes, until mushrooms soften.

Add the tomatoes with their juice, oregano, basil, red pepper, and salt and pepper to taste. Add honey, reduce heat to low, and simmer for about 30 minutes, stirring occasionally. Stir in the baby spinach and cook until wilted (just a few minutes).

When the roasted squash is cool enough to handle, slice it in half lengthwise and scoop out the seeds. Use a fork to scrape out the squash in long strands. Place in a serving dish, ladle sauce on top, and sprinkle with Parmesan cheese if desired.

SIDES, SOUPS, AND SALADS

Sweet Potato Fries

Makes 4 servings.

Ingredients

2 medium sweet potatoes
3 tablespoons olive oil
2 teaspoons kosher salt

Preheat oven to 450°F. Wash the sweet potatoes. Leave the peels on and slice them into ½" thick strips. In a mixing bowl, toss with the olive oil and salt.

Arrange in a single layer on a baking sheet. Bake for 15 minutes, flip, and bake for another 15 minutes.

Sweet potatoes are a particularly rich source of Vitamin A and also contain Vitamin E. A lot of the nutrients are just under the skin, so give the potatoes a good scrub and then leave the skins on.

Easy Lentil Stew

Makes 4 servings.

Ingredients

2 tablespoons olive oil
½ yellow onion, peeled
 and chopped
1 medium carrot, chopped
1½ cups dry lentils
4 cups chicken or
 vegetable broth
1 (14.5-ounce) can
 chopped tomatoes
1 medium potato, peeled
 and chopped into bite-
 sized chunks
1 tablespoon dried parsley
1 teaspoon cumin
Salt and pepper to taste

Rinse the lentils in a fine-mesh strainer.

In a stock pot or saucepan, heat the olive oil. Add the onions and carrots and sauté about 3 minutes, or until soft. Add all the remaining ingredients, cover, and simmer, stirring occasionally, for about 45 minutes, or until lentils and vegetables are tender. Taste and add more salt or pepper as desired.

Chai-Infused Coconut Milk Butternut Squash Soup

Makes 4 servings.

Ingredients

2 tablespoons butter or coconut oil

1 medium butternut squash

¼ cup minced yellow onion

1 tablespoon honey or maple syrup

½ teaspoon salt

½ teaspoon pepper

2 cups coconut milk

1 chai tea bag

Peel and seed the squash and cut into ½" chunks. In a stock pot or Dutch oven, melt the butter or coconut oil over medium heat. Add the squash and onion and sauté until squash is just barely tender, about 8 minutes. Add the honey or maple syrup, salt, and pepper, and sauté another couple of minutes.

Add the coconut milk, 3 cups of water, and the tea bag. Bring to a boil and then reduce heat and allow soup to simmer about 20 minutes.

Remove the tea bag and discard. Use an immersion blender to purée the soup. Alternately, you can use a blender or food processor, but you'll probably need to do a small portion at a time.

Taste and add additional salt and pepper as desired.

Tom Kha Gai Soup

Makes 6 servings.

Ingredients

1 (13.5-ounce) can coconut
  milk
2 cups chicken broth
1 tablespoon lemon juice
1" fresh ginger root,
  peeled and thinly sliced
1 pound boneless, skinless
  chicken breast
5 ounces baby bella
  mushrooms
2 tablespoons chopped
  fresh cilantro, plus more
  for garnish
⅛ teaspoon red pepper
  flakes

In a medium saucepan or stockpot, combine the coconut milk, chicken broth, lemon juice, and ginger root. Simmer over medium heat. Slice the chicken into 1" pieces and add to the broth mixture. Cook for about five minutes, or until the chicken is cooked through.

Add the mushrooms, cilantro, and red pepper flakes and simmer another 2–3 minutes. Remove from heat and transfer to a serving dish or bowls. Garnish with fresh cilantro and serve.

Sweet Potato Coconut Rice

Makes 6 servings.

Ingredients

2 cups brown rice
1 (13.5-ounce) can (2 cups)
   coconut milk
1½ cups water
1 medium sweet potato
½ teaspoon salt
⅛ teaspoon cinnamon
⅛ teaspoon ginger
⅛ teaspoon cloves
½ cup dried cranberries

In a rice cooker or pot with a lid over very low heat, stir together the rice, coconut milk, and water. Cover and simmer until rice is soft, about 20 minutes in a pot (or follow rice cooker instructions).

Meanwhile, chop the sweet potato into small chunks and cook in a pot of boiling water for about ten minutes or until a fork can easily stick into the pieces. Drain.

Fluff the rice with a fork and add sweet potato chunks and all remaining ingredients. Serve warm.

Curried Cauliflower Purée

Makes 6 servings.

Ingredients

1 head cauliflower (about 2 pounds)

2 tablespoons coconut oil (or unsalted butter)

2 tablespoons Greek yogurt

2 teaspoons curry powder

½ teaspoon salt

½ teaspoon pepper

Wash the cauliflower, trim off the leaves, and cut the stalk and florets into 1" chunks. Boil or steam the cauliflower until soft.

Drain the cauliflower (if you boiled it rather than steamed) and transfer to a mixing bowl. Add the remaining ingredients and purée with an immersion blender. Alternately, you can use a food processor or a hand masher. If too dry, add a little water or more yogurt.

When my husband served this to me recently, he smeared it elegantly across one side of the plate. Displayed this way, it makes an excellent base on which to place a neat stack of contrasting colored vegetables (steamed carrots or sautéed kale) or meat. It can also be served in a dollop, just like you would mashed potatoes.

Quinoa, Kale, and Pomegranate Salad

Makes 4–6 servings.

Ingredients

For the Salad

½ cup quinoa, uncooked

1 cup chicken or vegetable broth

1 large bunch lacinato kale

½ cup pomegranate seeds

½ cup sliced almonds

¼ cup crumbled goat cheese (optional)

For the Dressing

¾ cup cranberry or pomegranate juice

1 teaspoon apple cider vinegar

2 tablespoons extra virgin olive oil

Salt and pepper to taste

In a medium saucepan, combine quinoa and broth and bring to a boil. Reduce heat, cover, and allow to simmer for 15 minutes. Turn off heat, remove lid, and set aside to cool.

Wash the kale, pat it dry, discard stems, cut into long, thin strips, and place in a salad bowl. Add the pomegranate seeds, almonds, and goat cheese, if using. Scoop the cooled quinoa onto the salad and toss to mix.

Whisk all dressing ingredients together and pour over salad. Toss to mix.

This is a festive salad that's perfect for the holidays, but delicious any time of year. Red quinoa works nicely, but any variety will do. For the dressing, try to find juice that is only sweetened with fruit juices. If the dressing is too strong for your taste, add a little honey or maple syrup.

Creamy Teff Polenta

Makes 4–6 servings.

Ingredients

3 cups chicken or
   vegetable broth
½ teaspoon salt
½ teaspoon dried thyme
1 cup whole grain teff
1 tablespoon butter or
   coconut oil
¼ cup grated Parmesan

In a medium saucepan, bring the broth, salt, and thyme to a boil.

Add teff, stir, reduce heat to low, cover, and simmer about 20 minutes, or until water is absorbed and teff is tender.

Stir in butter or coconut oil and grated Parmesan.

Teff is a tiny, gluten-free grain that's native to Ethiopia. It's high in calcium, protein, and fiber. It can be ground into flour, but for this recipe, use the whole grain. Teff polenta makes a delicious, creamy base that can be topped with sautéed vegetables or tomato sauce for a full meal, or served as an accompaniment to meat dishes as you would mashed potatoes.

Cornbread Stuffing

Makes 6 servings.

Ingredients

1 pan pumpkin cornbread
(page 16)
1 small red onion, finely
chopped
1 stalk celery, finely
chopped
4 tablespoons butter
2 tablespoons olive oil
1 teaspoon Bell's poultry
seasoning
¼ teaspoon marjoram
¼ teaspoon thyme

Preheat oven to 350°F. Cut the cornbread into small cubes. Allow to sit out, uncovered, about 24 hours (this is optional—if you don't have time, fresh cornbread will work okay).

Melt 1 tablespoon butter in a frying pan (cast iron works well). Sauté onions and celery until onions begin to brown. Mix together with the cornbread. Mix the poultry seasoning with 1 cup hot water and pour over the cornbread mixture.

Grease an 8" x 8" baking pan and put the mixture in it. Melt the remaining butter with the olive oil and pour over top. Bake uncovered for about 20 minutes or until center is set and top is slightly crisp.

Herbed Digestive Biscuits

Makes about a dozen crackers.

Ingredients

1 cup brown rice flour
1 cup almond flour or
   other favorite gluten-free
   flour
½ teaspoons sea salt
1½ tablespoons olive oil
1 egg
Herbs or other seasonings
   to taste

Preheat oven to 350°F.

In a large bowl, mix together the flour and sea salt.

Whisk together olive oil and egg and add to dry ingredients, stirring until mixture forms coarse crumbs. Roll the dough into a ball. If it won't hang together, add another ½ teaspoon olive oil.

Cover a surface with parchment paper and put the ball of dough on it, placing another sheet of parchment paper on top. Roll out the dough to ⅛" thickness.

Transfer to a baking sheet and peel away the top layer of paper, leaving the bottom one so the crackers won't stick to the pan.

Sprinkle fresh or dried herbs, grated cheese, cinnamon-sugar, or other seasonings over the top. Cut into squares.

Bake for about fifteen minutes or until the crackers begin to brown. Remove from the oven and allow to cool for several minutes before transferring to a cooling rack.

Digestive biscuits, beloved in England, are softer than crackers and not as sweet as cookies. To make these more traditional, use a round cookie cutter to cut the dough before baking. You can experiment with different gluten-free flour combinations. Try buckwheat, cornmeal, oat flour, or amaranth for slightly different flavors and textures.

Yogurt Cheese

Makes about 5 ounces of cheese.

Ingredients
1 pint plain yogurt
⅛ teaspoon salt
  (if desired)
Fresh or dried herbs,
  black pepper, or other
  seasonings to taste

Equipment
Medium-sized bowl
Strainer
Cheesecloth
Scissors

Rest your strainer inside the bowl. The rim of the bowl should be slightly smaller than the circumference of the strainer so that the strainer is suspended at least an inch away from the bottom of the bowl.

Cut about 2 square feet of cheesecloth and fold it in half so that it's double the thickness. Line the strainer with the cheesecloth.

If using salt, add it to the yogurt and pour the mixture into the center of the cheesecloth. Pull the edges of the cloth together to make a neat bundle. You can tie the bundle if you want, but usually the cloth will stick to itself fairly easily.

Place in the refrigerator for a few hours or overnight. The liquid will gradually seep out of the yogurt and leave you with a soft, creamy cheese. To serve, turn the cheesecloth over onto a plate or board and sprinkle with herbs or other garnish.

Yogurt cheese is soft (similar to cream cheese) and has a sharp flavor that can be spruced up with fresh or dried herbs, finely chopped nuts, black pepper, or a drizzle of honey for a sweet variation. I like to use plain whole milk yogurt, as it yields a smooth, rich cheese. You can use the nutritious leftover yogurt liquid that drains out in smoothies or soups.

Dill Yogurt Dip

Makes 2 cups.

Ingredients
2 cups Greek yogurt
¼ cup chopped fresh dill
½ teaspoon kosher salt

Mix all ingredients together and serve with gluten-free crackers or pita.

Greek yogurt is just regular yogurt that has drained for longer, making it extra thick and creamy. It's great for a sour cream substitute in any dip or spread. Yogurt is full of good bacteria that aids in digestion and immunity. Compared to regular yogurt ounce per ounce, Greek yogurt is higher in protein and lower in lactose and sugars.

Tahini and Herb Potato Salad

Makes 6 servings.

Ingredients

2 pounds potatoes (red, yellow, or new potatoes), washed and chopped into bite-sized chunks
1 cup frozen peas
½ cup Greek yogurt
2 tablespoons lemon juice
2 teaspoons honey
2 teaspoons tahini
¼ cup chopped fresh mint, parsley, or oregano (or a combination)
Sea salt and black pepper to taste

Place the potato chunks in a large pot, fill with water until potatoes are covered, and place over medium-high heat. Bring to a boil and cook until potatoes are just tender (about 10 minutes). Add the peas, cook another minute, and then drain in a colander and rinse with cold water. Transfer to a serving dish.

In a small bowl, mix together all remaining ingredients and pour over potatoes and peas. Mix to coat. Taste and add additional salt or pepper if desired. Refrigerate until ready to serve.

Roasted Vegetables

Makes 6 servings.

Ingredients

2 medium potatoes (yellow or red), washed and chopped into chunks

2 sweet potatoes, washed and chopped into chunks

1 red onion, quartered

1 medium carrot, washed and chopped into chunks

1 apple, washed, cored, and chopped into chunks

2 teaspoons fresh thyme

1 tablespoon fresh rosemary

3 tablespoons olive oil

2 tablespoons balsamic vinegar

1 tablespoon gluten-free tamari

¼ teaspoon cinnamon

2 garlic cloves, peeled and minced

Pinch of sea salt and black pepper, to taste

Preheat oven to 475°F. Combine all the veggies and the apple in a large bowl. Add remaining ingredients and toss to coat.

Spread on a large roasting pan and roast for 35–40 minutes, or until veggies are soft, stirring every 10 minutes or so.

Cider-Glazed Carrots

Makes 4–6 servings.

Ingredients

3 cups fresh carrots, washed and sliced into strips
2 tablespoons butter or coconut oil
1 tablespoon honey
½ cup apple cider
3 tablespoons water
¼ teaspoon cinnamon
⅛ teaspoon cloves

In a large skillet, sauté carrots in butter or coconut oil over medium heat for about 5 minutes.

Add the remaining ingredients and bring to a boil. Reduce heat to low, cover, and simmer for about 10 minutes, or until carrots are just barely tender.

Transfer to a serving dish or arrange on plates to serve.

Millet Corn Fritters

Makes about 15 fritters.

Ingredients

½ cup millet flour
½ cup brown rice flour
¼ teaspoon salt
2 teaspoons baking
  powder
1 tablespoon olive oil, plus
  additional for frying
⅔ cup milk (dairy, coconut,
  almond, or soy)
1 egg, beaten
1 teaspoon honey or
  maple syrup
1 (15.25-ounce) can corn

In a medium mixing bowl, whisk together the flours, salt, and baking powder.

In a separate bowl, whisk together the olive oil, milk, egg, and honey or maple syrup. Add the wet ingredients to the dry and stir to combine. Drain the corn and fold into batter.

Heat a skillet on medium-high and add a little olive oil to lightly coat the bottom of the pan. Drop spoonfuls of batter onto the skillet, frying a couple of minutes on each side until fritters are golden. Transfer to a plate lined with a paper towel. Repeat until all batter is used. You can keep fritters hot in the oven set to low heat.

Serve hot with butter, maple syrup, or applesauce. These are also delicious topped with sliced tomatoes and a small dollop of Greek yogurt. Millet corn fritters can be made with all millet flour instead of half millet and half brown rice. However, millet has a very strong flavor that I find is better when tempered with a more neutral-tasting flour.

These could easily have been in the breakfast and breads section of this book, but they make such a great accompaniment to both sweet and savory dishes of all kinds that I didn't want to pigeon hole them as a breakfast food.

Grilled Pear Salad with Green Tea Dressing

Makes 4 servings as a side salad.

Ingredients

Dressing

½ cup strong-brewed
 green tea
2 tablespoons grapeseed oil
1 tablespoon unfiltered
 apple cider vinegar
2 tablespoons honey
1 tablespoon gluten-free
 tamari
½ teaspoon salt

Pears

2 firm pears, halved and
 seeded
2 tablespoons honey

Salad

4 cups arugula, rinsed and
 patted or spun dry
1 tablespoon coconut oil
 or butter
¾ cups shelled walnut halves

Preheat oven to 375°F.

To make the dressing, combine all ingredients in a food processor or shake in a jar.

Place pear halves on a baking sheet, cut side up, and brush the cut sides with honey. Bake for about 20 minutes, or until lightly browned. Cut into thin slices.

In a skillet, heat the coconut oil or butter and sauté the walnut halves until lightly toasted, just a few minutes.

Toss the arugula, pear slices, and toasted walnuts together with desired amount of dressing. If you don't use all the dressing, keep it in the refrigerator for another salad.

Summer Rolls with Peanut Dipping Sauce

Makes 5 rolls.

Ingredients

10 rice paper rounds
   (6" or 8" in diameter)
5 lettuce leaves
1 carrot, coarsely shredded
Small bunch fresh cilantro
Small bunch fresh mint
1 Haas avocado, halved,
   pitted, and cut into thin
   wedges

Dipping Sauce:
¼ cup peanut butter
2 tablespoons gluten-free
   tamari
1 tablespoon rice wine
1 tablespoon brown sugar
1 teaspoon freshly grated
   ginger

Fill a pie plate with warm water and lay a towel flat on the work surface beside it. Dip one rice paper round in the warm water and allow to soften (it'll just take a few seconds). Remove and lay flat on the towel. Repeat with a second round, laying it directly on top of the first rice paper round. Pat the top dry with a paper towel.

Place a lettuce leaf in the center of the rice paper. Arrange the carrot, avocado, and a few leaves of the cilantro and mint in a neat line across the lettuce, using less than you think you need and leaving about an inch of space around the edges.

Fold in the sides and then roll up the whole thing into a log. Slice in half on a diagonal and serve with dipping sauce.

To make the sauce, whisk together the ingredients and then add a teaspoon or two of water to thin it out.

Baked Mushroom Quesadillas

Serves 4–6 as an appetizer.

Ingredients

2 tablespoons olive oil, divided

5 ounces mushrooms, sliced

2 teaspoons balsamic vinegar

3 tablespoons goat cheese

6 corn tortillas

1 cup shredded mozzarella

Heat the olive oil in a sauté pan and add the mushrooms. Sauté until mushrooms are tender, about 5 minutes, and add the balsamic vinegar and goat cheese. Cook another few minutes, stirring regularly. Remove from heat.

Heat the oven to 425°F. Place three tortillas on a baking sheet. Place a few tablespoons of the mushroom filling in the center of each tortilla, sprinkle some shredded mozzarella on top, and place another tortilla on top of each. Bake for about 5 minutes or until cheese is fully melted. Remove from oven and cut in halves or quarters.

DESSERTS

Oatmeal Peppermint Chip Cookies

Makes about 2 dozen cookies.

Ingredients

½ cup butter or coconut
  oil
½ cup brown sugar
¼ cup white sugar
1 egg
1 teaspoon peppermint
  extract
½ teaspoon baking soda
2½ cups oat flour
½ teaspoon salt
¾ cup chocolate chips

Allow the butter or coconut oil to soften to room temperature. Beat together with the sugars, egg, and peppermint extract.

In a medium bowl, whisk together the oat flour, baking soda, and salt. Add to the wet ingredients and stir until combined. Add the chocolate chips and stir until incorporated.

Drop by teaspoonfuls onto an ungreased cookie sheet, leaving ample space between each one as cookies will spread significantly. Bake about 10 minutes or until edges are golden. Cookies will still be soft, but remove from oven and allow to cool. Don't worry, they'll firm up as they cool.

You can easily make oat flour in a food processor—just dump in the oats and let it whirl until the oats become a flour consistency.

Vegan Pumpkin Brownies

Makes about 16 brownies.

Ingredients

1 cup all-purpose
gluten-free flour (page 3)
1 cup oat flour
1 cup white sugar
¾ cup unsweetened cocoa
powder
1 teaspoon baking powder
1 teaspoon salt
1 cup fruit juice (apple is
great, but any variety
will do)
¼ cup vegetable oil
1 cup pumpkin purée
½ cup applesauce
1 teaspoon vanilla extract
1 cup chocolate chips

Preheat the oven to 350°F. Grease a 9" x 13" baking pan.

In a medium-sized mixing bowl, stir together the flours, sugar, cocoa powder, baking powder, and salt. Pour in juice, vegetable oil, pumpkin purée, applesauce, and vanilla. Mix until well blended.

Spread evenly in baking pan. Sprinkle chocolate chips evenly over the top.

Bake for 25 to 30 minutes or until the top is no longer shiny. Let cool for at least 10 minutes before cutting into squares.

Maple Bananas Flambé

Makes 4 servings.

3 large bananas
3 tablespoons butter or
  coconut oil
¼ cup maple syrup
½ teaspoon cinnamon

Peel the bananas and chop at an angle into ½" chunks.

Melt the butter or coconut oil in a skillet and add the banana chunks. Sauté over medium heat for about 2 minutes. Add the maple syrup and cinnamon and sauté, stirring, until syrup begins to caramelize (about a minute). Serve hot alone or over ice cream or frozen yogurt.

Raspberry Peach Cobbler

Makes 8–10 servings.

Ingredients

5 medium peaches,
  peeled and sliced
2 cups fresh or frozen
  raspberries
1 tablespoon cornstarch
¾ cup gluten-free oats
¾ cup all-purpose gluten-
  free flour (page 3)
1 cup brown sugar
1 teaspoon cinnamon
½ teaspoon nutmeg
1 stick (½ cup) butter, cut
  into pieces

Preheat oven to 350°F.

In a large bowl, mix together peach slices, raspberries, and cornstarch. Divide between 8–10 ramekins. In a medium mixing bowl, combine oats, flour, brown sugar, cinnamon, and nutmeg. Mix the butter in, using two forks, a pastry cutter, or your fingers to incorporate.

Place ramekins on a cookie sheet and divide topping between them. Bake for 35–40 minutes, or until topping is golden and bubbly. Cool before serving so that ramekins don't burn your fingers.

Rather than baking in ramekins, you can bake in a 2-quart casserole dish or a deep pie plate and then scoop into tea cups to serve.

Rustic Plum Galettes

Makes about 6 galettes.

Ingredients

Pastry

1½ cups all-purpose
    gluten-free flour (page 3)
½ cup almond flour
2 teaspoons xanthan gum
¼ teaspoon salt
2 tablespoons sugar
8 tablespoons coconut oil,
    soft but not liquid
2 teaspoons cider vinegar
6–8 tablespoons ice water

Plum Filling

¼ cup maple syrup or honey
3 tablespoons ground
    almonds
1 tablespoon cornstarch
½ cup plum, apricot, or
    raspberry preserves
2 tablespoons coconut oil
2 pounds fresh plums, pitted
    and sliced into thin wedges

In a food processor, combine flour, almond flour, xanthan gum, salt, and sugar and pulse to mix. Add the coconut oil and pulse until coarse crumbs form. Add cider and 4 tablespoons water, pulse, and then add 1 tablespoon water at a time until dough hangs together. Place a large piece of parchment paper on a flat work surface, form dough into a ball, and place the ball on top of the paper. Cover with another large piece of parchment paper and roll out to about ⅛" thick. Refrigerate for about 20 minutes.

Mix together the maple syrup or honey, ground almonds, cornstarch, and preserves in a small mixing bowl.

When the dough is chilled, preheat oven to 375°F. Cut the dough into circles about 4" in diameter and arrange on a baking sheet. Gather dough scraps and repeat.

Spread the dough rounds with the filling mixture, leaving a 1" border. Dot with coconut oil, and then arrange a few plum slices on each one. Fold up the pastry edges, pressing lightly to adhere as necessary.

Bake for 40–45 minutes, or until pastry is golden. Remove from oven and cool on wire racks.

Make sure the coconut oil is soft but not liquid when you use it. If it's too hard, heat it briefly until it softens up. If it's too liquidy, chill it before use.

Amaranth Cracker Jacks

Makes about 4 cups.

¾ cup amaranth
2 tablespoons honey or
  maple syrup
2 tablespoons coconut oil
  or butter
1 cup cashews
1 cup almonds
½ cup dried cranberries
¼ teaspoon coarse sea salt

To pop the amaranth, first heat a medium pot over high heat. To test that the pan is hot enough, add a drop of water. If it quickly forms a ball and evaporates, the pot is the right temperature.

Add 2 tablespoons of amaranth to the pot, cover with a lid, and gently shake the pot, sliding it back and forth in quick movements just above the burner. Within 10 to 15 seconds the amaranth should be fully popped. Be careful not to burn!

Empty popped amaranth into a bowl and repeat until all amaranth is popped.

Preheat oven to 275°F.

Combine popped amaranth with the nuts and dried cranberries. In a small saucepan, melt together the sweetener and coconut oil or butter. Pour over the amaranth mixture, add salt, and stir to coat. Place on a parchment paper–lined cookie sheet and bake for about half an hour, stirring with a spatula every 10 minutes or so.

Allow cracker jacks to cool completely before storing in an airtight container.

Mango Yogurt Ice Pops

Makes 8 pops.

Ingredients

1 cup mango juice
1 cup fresh or frozen
   mango chunks
1 (6-ounce) container
   vanilla yogurt
8 wooden popsicle sticks

Combine all ingredients in blender and blend until smooth. Pour into 8 popsicle molds. Cover, insert popsicle sticks, and freeze at least 2 hours.

To serve, run hot water over bottoms of molds to loosen the popsicles. To display at a gathering, arrange popsicles in a bucket of ice or frozen berries. Wrap leftover popsicles individually in plastic wrap and store in a sealed freezer bag in the freezer.

Dairy-Free Chocolate Cherry Popsicles

Makes 8 popsicles.

Ingredients

1 (13.5-ounce) can coconut
milk
4 tablespoons honey
1 teaspoon vanilla or
almond extract
2 tablespoons coconut oil
1 cup frozen cherries,
thawed and chopped
into small pieces
3 ounces dark chocolate,
finely chopped
(about ½ cup)

Combine coconut milk, honey, vanilla, and coconut oil in a blender and blend until smooth and creamy. Pour a little into the bottom of each of 8 popsicle molds. Add a layer of cherry pieces, then chocolate chunks, then more of the liquid. Continue until all ingredients are used, finishing with the liquid. Freeze at least 3 hours.

To serve, run hot water over bottoms of molds to loosen the popsicles. To display at a gathering, arrange popsicles in a bucket of ice. Wrap leftover popsicles individually in plastic wrap and store in a sealed freezer bag in the freezer.

Chickpea Chocolate Chip Cookies

Makes about a dozen cookies.

Ingredients

1 (15-ounce) can chickpeas, rinsed and thoroughly drained
¾ cup peanut butter
1 teaspoon vanilla
2 tablespoons brewed coffee
¼ cup maple syrup or honey
1 teaspoon baking powder
5 ounces (½ bag) chocolate chips

Preheat oven to 350°F.

Combine all ingredients except chocolate chips in a food processer and process until smooth. Add chocolate chips and stir.

Drop by teaspoonfuls onto a cookie sheet lined with parchment paper.

Bake for about ten minutes. Cookies will still be soft.

The first time I was experimenting with these cookies there was a little leftover coffee in my French press and I decided to add a splash to the batter. I loved the flavor it added, but if you don't have coffee around, you can use milk, fruit juice, or even just water.

Sugar Plums

Makes about a dozen.

Ingredients

½ cup almonds,
  hazelnuts, or walnuts (or
  a mix)
¾ cup Medjool
  dates, prunes, dried
  cranberries, or raisins
  (or a mix)
1 tablespoon honey
3 tablespoons nut butter
  (almond, peanut, or
  cashew)
⅛ teaspoon almond
  extract
⅛ teaspoon vanilla
½ teaspoon cinnamon
⅛ teaspoon cloves
½ cup raw, coarse sugar

In a food processor, pulse together the dried fruit and nuts. Add the remaining ingredients except for the sugar and pulse until mixture starts to clump together.

Roll the dough into small balls and roll in the sugar.

Raspberry Sorbet

Makes about 1 pint.

Ingredients

1 cup water
½ cup sugar
2 cups fresh raspberries
Juice of ½ lemon (around
   2 tablespoons)

Combine all ingredients in a saucepan and bring to a boil, stirring to avoid burning. Boil 3–4 minutes and then simmer an additional 10 minutes, allowing raspberries to break down.

After mixture cools, blend well with an immersion blender. Strain through mesh strainer (or through colander lined with cheesecloth if you don't have a mesh strainer), pressing on the solids.

Chill purée for 1 hour or until cold, or quick chill in a bowl of ice and cold water, stirring occasionally, for 15 to 20 minutes (until cold).

Freeze purée in ice-cream maker according to directions. Garnish with berries if desired.

Easy Coconut Mango Blender Sorbet

Makes about 3 cups.

Ingredients

2 cups frozen mango
chunks
½ cup unsweetened
coconut milk
¼ cup honey or maple
syrup
Dash cinnamon
Dash nutmeg

Combine all ingredients in a blender and blend until smooth. Enjoy immediately or store in a metal or glass dish in the freezer.

If your blender is not very powerful, you may need to combine ingredients in a bowl and then blend a little at a time, or add more liquid. Experiment with different frozen fruits to create your own sorbet recipe. Bananas, raspberries, and blueberries are great options. You can also use soy, almond, or cow's milk instead of coconut milk. For an elegant presentation, serve sorbet in hollowed-out citrus peels or coconut shells.

Candied Orange Peels

Makes about 1 cup of candy.

Ingredients

3 oranges (peels only)
5 cups sugar, divided
3 cups water

In a large saucepan, bring 3 cups of water to a boil. Wash the orange peels and slice them into strips ¼" wide. Place in the boiling water and cook for 15 minutes. Drain into a colander and rinse the peels.

In the saucepan whisk together 3 cups of water with 4 cups of sugar. Bring to a boil over medium heat. Add the peels and simmer over low heat for about 45 minutes

Drain into a colander, reserving the syrup for other uses. Place 1 cup of sugar in a bowl and toss the peels until well coated.

Transfer peels to a baking sheet lined with aluminum foil. Let stand for 1 to 2 days or until coating is dried. Extras can be stored in the freezer for up to 2 months.

Chocolate-Dipped Fruit Skewers

Makes about 6 skewers—may be more or less depending on type of fruit.

Ingredients

6 ounces semisweet or
  dark chocolate, chopped
1 pound berries,
  pineapple, bananas,
  dried apricots, or any
  other fruit
⅛ to ¼ teaspoon spices
  (optional) such as
  cinnamon, cayenne,
  cardamom, or ginger
Toppings (optional) such
  as coarse sugar, cacao
  nibs, sprinkles, or
  crushed nuts
Wooden skewers

Wash fruit and pat dry. Berries can stay whole, but larger fruit should be chopped into bite-sized pieces.

Melt chocolate in a double boiler. Add spice, if using, and stir with spatula. Keep heat on low.

Pierce each piece of fruit with a skewer and dip in the chocolate. Roll the fruit in your desired topping and place on a cookie sheet lined with parchment paper. Chocolate will set within a few minutes. Extras can be stored in the refrigerator.

Chocolate-dipped fruit lends an elegant touch to any gathering. You can use fresh or dried fruit for this recipe (no need to wash dried fruit before dipping).

Grilled Peaches with Maple Cinnamon Yogurt

Make 4 servings.

Ingredients

4 peaches
3 tablespoons maple
   syrup, divided
½ cup Greek-style yogurt
¼ teaspoon ground
   cinnamon

Heat greased grill to medium-high.

Mix together the yogurt, 1 tablespoon of the maple syrup, and the cinnamon. Set aside.

Wash the peaches, slice them in half, and remove the pits. Brush the cut sides with the remaining maple syrup. Grill cut-side down 6–8 minutes or until softened. Top with a dollop of the yogurt and serve immediately.

Honey can be substituted for maple syrup and will also be delicious!

Dates Stuffed with Goat Cheese and Chocolate

Makes 24 candies.

Ingredients

24 whole pitted Medjool
  dates
¼ cup goat cheese
2 teaspoons unsweetened
  cocoa powder
3 teaspoons confectioners'
  sugar

Cut a slit along the length of each date. In a small bowl, mix together the goat cheese, cocoa powder, and 1 teaspoon confectioners' sugar. Place a small scoop of the mixture inside each date.

Sift remaining confectioners' sugar over the tops of the dates. Serve immediately or store in the refrigerator for up to a few days.

Apricot-Orange Balls

Makes about 24 balls.

Ingredients

1 cup dried apricots or peaches

⅔ cup lightly toasted nuts (hazelnuts, walnuts, almonds, or pecans work well)

3 tablespoons honey

2 teaspoons grated orange zest

2 tablespoons orange juice or rum

3 ounces bittersweet chocolate

In a food processor, pulse apricots and nuts just until finely chopped. Scoop mixture into a bowl and add honey, orange zest, and orange juice. Roll mixture into 1" balls and set on a parchment paper–lined baking sheet.

Melt chocolate in a double boiler. Drizzle chocolate over tops of the balls in a zig-zag pattern. Refrigerate for about 30 minutes. Store in airtight container in refrigerator up to 2 weeks.

Typically a holiday treat, these easy confections can be whipped up and enjoyed any time of year. Make ahead and store in the refrigerator and then pull them out and display in a candy dish for an easy party treat.

Coconut Rice Pudding

Makes about 8 small servings.

Ingredients

1 cup brown rice,
uncooked
2 cups coconut milk,
divided
¼ cup maple syrup or
honey
¼ teaspoon salt
1 egg, beaten
½ cup raisins
1 tablespoon coconut oil
1 teaspoon vanilla
1 teaspoon cinnamon

In a medium saucepan, bring 1½ cups water to a boil. Add rice, stir, cover, reduce heat to low, and simmer for 20 minutes.

In a clean saucepan, combine cooked rice, 1½ cups coconut milk, maple syrup or honey, and salt. Cover and cook over medium heat for about 20 minutes. Add remaining ½ cup coconut milk, beaten egg, and raisins, and stir. Cook for another 3 minutes, stirring regularly.

Remove from heat and add coconut oil, vanilla, and cinnamon, stirring until incorporated. Cover and refrigerate until ready to serve.

Coconut Milk Truffles

Makes about 30 truffles.

Ingredients

10 ounces semisweet or
   dark chocolate, chopped
   into small bits
1 cup (about ½ can) full-fat
   coconut milk
2 tablespoons coconut oil
1 teaspoon vanilla
½ teaspoon cinnamon
Cocoa powder, crushed
   nuts, or coconut flakes
   for coating

Place the chocolate pieces in a medium-sized mixing bowl. In a small saucepan, heat the coconut milk and the coconut oil until it begins to simmer, and then pour over the chocolate. Add the vanilla and cinnamon and stir until the mixture becomes smooth. Refrigerate for about 2 hours.

Line a baking sheet with parchment paper. Remove the ganache mixture from the refrigerator. Scoop out small spoonfuls of the ganache and then roll between your palms to form smooth balls. Place on the lined baking sheet and refrigerate for another 30 minutes.

Roll the balls in the coating of your choice and serve. Store in the refrigerator in an airtight container.

Fruit Leather

Makes 6 to 8 servings.

Ingredients

3 cups applesauce or other
   puréed fruit
2 tablespoons honey
⅛ teaspoon salt

Line a rimmed baking sheet with parchment paper or a silicone baking mat. Heat oven to 170°F.

Mix ingredients together and then pour onto the lined baking sheet. Spread evenly with a rubber spatula. Bake for 6–7 hours.

When the fruit mixture is sufficiently leathery, remove from oven and allow to cool. Remove paper and cut into shapes or strips. Store between layers of parchment paper up to 3 weeks.

If you have a food dehydrator, use that instead of your oven for this recipe!

If you decide to use raspberries, strawberries, or any fruit that contains small seeds, push purée through a strainer to remove seeds before baking.

Experiment with adding a dash of cinnamon, ginger, orange zest, or other spices or flavorings.

Crystallized Ginger

Makes 1 pound.

Ingredients

1 pound fresh ginger root, peeled and sliced ⅛" thick

4 cups granulated sugar, plus some for coating

4 cups water

Place the peeled and sliced ginger in a saucepan with the water and sugar, stir, and simmer over medium–high heat for about half an hour.

With a slotted spoon, scoop out the ginger and place on a wire rack. Allow to dry and then toss ginger in additional granulated sugar.

Store in an airtight container.

Zingy and slightly chewy, crystallized ginger can help to alleviate nausea and generally aid digestion. Reserve the liquid from the recipe for use in Honey Lemon Ginger Drops (page 121) or for use in homemade ginger ale!

Honey Lemon Ginger Drops

Makes a little less than a pound of drops.

Ingredients
½ cup water
3" piece of ginger root, peeled and finely diced
1 cup honey
2 tablespoons apple cider vinegar
2 teaspoons fresh-squeezed lemon juice
½ teaspoon slippery elm powder (optional)

Line a cookie sheet with parchment paper and spray lightly with cooking spray.

In a small saucepan over low heat, simmer the water and ginger for about half an hour. Strain, reserving the liquid. (You can toss the ginger bits in sugar, let them dry on a cookie sheet, and enjoy them as chewy ginger candies.)

In a medium saucepan, combine the ginger water, honey, and vinegar. Stir with a metal spoon until honey liquefies.

Stop stirring and insert the candy thermometer. Don't stir the syrup again until it's removed from the heat. Allow mixture to come to a boil. If sugar crystals form on the sides of the pan, wipe them away with a damp pastry brush.

When the syrup reaches 300°F, remove from heat. If you're not using a candy thermometer, this is hard crack stage. Allow mixture to cool slightly until boiling has ceased. Add the lemon juice and stir.

Working quickly, use a ½ teaspoon measure to drop the syrup onto the lined cookie sheet, leaving a little space between each one. If desired, sprinkle with slippery elm powder. Let cool for at least a half hour. Store for about a week at room temperature or refrigerate for longer storage.

Cherry and Dark Chocolate Biscotti

Makes about a dozen biscotti.

Ingredients

¾ cup oat flour

¾ cup all-purpose gluten-
free flour (page 3)

½ teaspoon xanthan gum

½ cup brown sugar

⅛ teaspoon salt

1½ teaspoons baking
powder

½ teaspoon cinnamon

2 eggs

2 ½ tablespoons olive oil

2 teaspoons vanilla

½ cup dried cherries

¼ cup dark chocolate
chips

¼ cup sliced almonds

Heat oven to 350°F and grease a baking sheet. In a medium mixing bowl, whisk together the first seven ingredients. In a separate bowl, whisk the two eggs. Place 2 tablespoons of the eggs into a separate dish and set aside. Whisk the olive oil and vanilla into the remaining eggs.

Pour egg, oil, and vanilla mixture into the dry mixture and stir to combine. Fold in the dried cherries and chocolate chips.

Dust a surface with gluten-free flour and roll out the dough to about ½" thickness. Use hands to shape it into a rectangle. Brush with the remaining egg and sprinkle with sliced almonds.

Bake for about 30 minutes, or until top begins to brown. Remove from oven, reduce heat to 250°F, and allow biscotti to cool for about 15 minutes.

Transfer biscotti to a cutting board and use a serrated knife to slice into ½" wide strips. Place strips cut-side down on baking sheet and return to oven. Bake for 20 minutes, turn biscotti over, and bake another 20 minutes. Transfer biscotti to a wire rack to cool. Store in an airtight container.

Dried cherries can be expensive or difficult to find at all. Dried cranberries make a good substitute, or sometimes you can find cranberries infused with cherry juice, which are delicious!

GLUTEN-FREE MIXES

Gluten–Free Pancake Mix

Makes enough mix for 4 batches, or about 40 pancakes.

Ingredients

3 cups all-purpose gluten-free flour (page 3)

1 cup buckwheat or oat flour

¾ teaspoon xanthan gum

½ teaspoon salt

1 tablespoon baking powder

1½ teaspoons baking soda

¼ cup sugar

Mix all ingredients together thoroughly and pour into an airtight container or bag. A mason jar with a ribbon tied around the lid makes an attractive and reusable gift package.

Be sure to include these instructions with the mix: To make pancakes, stir together 1 cup pancake mix, 1 egg, 1 tablespoon butter or coconut oil, and 1¼ cups milk (almond, soy, coconut, dairy, or buttermilk). Allow batter to rest for several minutes. Meanwhile, heat the griddle and allow about 1 teaspoon of butter or coconut oil to melt on the surface. Use a spatula to make sure the whole surface of the griddle is greased. Pour about ¼ cup batter on the pan and cook pancakes for about 3 minutes on each side. Pancakes are done when they're dry on the outside and a little golden but not too brown. Makes about 10 pancakes.

Gluten-Free Mexican Brownie Mix

Makes enough mix to fill one pint jar and to make one 8" x 8" pan of brownies.

Ingredients

½ cup gluten-free
  all-purpose flour (page 3)
½ cup unsweetened cocoa
  powder
¼ teaspoon baking
  powder
¼ teaspoon salt
¾ cup sugar
½ teaspoon cinnamon
½ teaspoon chili powder
  or cayenne pepper

Stir together all the ingredients and pour into a glass pint jar or a sealable bag.

Include these directions with the mix: Preheat oven to 350°F and grease an 8" x 8" pan. Combine all of the mix with ½ cup unsalted butter or coconut oil, softened; 2 large eggs; and 1 teaspoon vanilla. Pour batter into prepared pan and bake for about 25 minutes. Cool in the pan for several minutes before cutting.

To make a regular brownie mix (instead of Mexican brownies), just omit the cinnamon and chili powder or cayenne pepper. You can also add ½ cup of chocolate chips to the mix for extra chocolaty brownies (though you may need a slightly larger jar to package it in).

Gluten-Free Muffin Mix

Makes mix for 12 regular muffins or 6 large muffins.

Ingredients

2 cups all-purpose gluten-
free flour (page 3)
½ teaspoon xanthan gum
½ teaspoon salt
1 tablespoon baking
powder
½ cup brown sugar
1 teaspoon cinnamon
½ teaspoon nutmeg
½ cup dried apples or
berries (optional)

Stir together all the ingredients and pour into a glass pint jar or a sealable bag.

Include these directions with the mix: Preheat oven to 400°F and grease a 12-cup muffin tin. Combine all of the mix with 4 tablespoons unsalted butter or coconut oil, melted; 2 large eggs; 1 cup milk; and 1 teaspoon vanilla. Mix just until combined. Pour batter into prepared pan and bake for about 20 minutes, or until a toothpick inserted into the center of a muffin comes out clean.

Gluten-Free Bread Machine Mix

Makes 1 loaf.

Ingredients

3 cups all-purpose gluten-free flour (page 3)

3½ teaspoons xanthan gum

¼ cup sugar

1 teaspoon salt

1 Vitamin C tablet, crushed

2¼ teaspoons active dry yeast

Combine all ingredients and package in a glass jar or airtight bag.

Include these instructions with the mix: Run three eggs under hot water for a minute or two or until eggs are room temperature. Whisk together the 3 large eggs, ¼ cup oil, and 1¼ cups milk (milk should be at room temperature). Pour into bread machine. Add mix and cook on light setting.

Gluten-Free Peanut Butter Cookie Mix

Makes mix for a dozen cookies.

Ingredients

1½ cups all-purpose
  gluten-free flour (page 3)
½ teaspoon baking soda
½ cup brown sugar
¼ cup white sugar
½ cup chocolate chips

Combine all ingredients and package in a glass jar or sealable bag.

Include these instructions with the mix: Preheat oven to 375°F. Combine the mix with ½ cup butter or coconut oil, 1 egg, 1 teaspoon vanilla, and ½ cup salted natural peanut butter. Roll dough into small balls and place 2" apart on a cookie sheet. Bake for about 8 minutes or until cookies hang together. Cool cookies on cookie sheet for a few minutes before transferring to a wire rack.

About the Author

Abigail R. Gehring has enjoyed cooking and experimenting in the kitchen since she was a child. In college, she assisted food writer and cookbook author Nina Simonds, who taught her how to properly chop ginger and garlic and filled her head with exciting notions of a life peppered with food writing and travel. Through that experience, she also had the opportunity to drive famed cookbook editor Judith Jones from Logon airport to Salem, Massachusetts—a drive full of conversations that got her thinking about writing possibilities and editing for exciting New York City publishing houses.

Now Abigail edits cookbooks and manages the art and production departments at Skyhorse Publishing in New York City. She is the author of more than a dozen books on cooking and country living skills. Since going gluten-free for health reasons in 2009, she has turned her focus to healthy gluten-free cooking.

Food photography is a more recent passion of Abigail's. With help from her husband, Tim Lawrence, she's had a wonderful time learning her way around a camera.

Abigail can't remember a time that she's followed a recipe exactly, except when she's testing her own for a cookbook. She divides her time between New York City and Chester, Vermont.

Conversion Charts

OVEN TEMPERATURES

Fahrenheit	Celcius	Gas Mark
225°	110°	¼
250°	120°	½
275°	140°	1
300°	150°	2
325°	160°	3
350°	180°	4
375°	190°	5
400°	200°	6
425°	220°	7
450°	230°	8

METRIC AND IMPERIAL CONVERSIONS

(These conversions are rounded for convenience)

Ingredient	Cups/Tablespoons/Teaspoons	Ounces	Grams/Milliliters
Amaranth, uncooked	1 cup	6.8 ounces	190 grams
Butter	1 cup=16 tablespoons= 2 sticks	8 ounces	230 grams
Cream cheese	1 tablespoon	0.5 ounces	14.5 grams
Cheese, shredded	1 cup	4 ounces	110 grams
Cornstarch	1 tablespoon	0.3 ounces	8 grams
Flour, all-purpose (gluten-free)	1 cup/1 tablespoon	4.5 ounces/0.3 ounces	125 grams/8 grams
Flour, buckwheat	1 cup	4.25 ounces	120 grams
Flour, sorghum	1 cup	4.25 ounces	120 grams
Fruit, dried	1 cup	4 ounces	120 grams
Fruits or veggies, chopped	1 cup	5 to 7 ounces	145 to 200 grams
Fruits or veggies, puréed	1 cup	8.5 ounces	245 grams
Honey or maple syrup,	1 tablespoon	.75 ounces	20 grams
Liquids: cream, milk, water, or juice	1 cup	8 fluid ounces	240 milliliters
Oats	1 cup	5.5 ounces	150 grams
Quinoa, uncooked	1 cup	6 ounces	170 grams
Salt	1 teaspoon	0.2 ounces	6 grams
Spices: cinnamon, cloves, ginger, or nutmeg (ground)	1 teaspoon	0.2 ounces	5 milliliters
Sugar, brown, firmly packed	1 cup	7 ounces	200 grams
Sugar, white	1 cup/1 tablespoon	7 ounces/0.5 ounces	200 grams/12.5 grams
Vanilla extract	1 teaspoon	0.2 ounces	4 grams

Index